Fyodor Dostoevsky

Titles in the series Critical Lives present the work of leading cultural figures of the modern period. Each book explores the life of the artist, writer, philosopher or architect in question and relates it to their major works.

Fyodor Dostoevsky

Robert Bird

REAKTION BOOKS

For Robert Louis Jackson

Published by Reaktion Books Ltd
33 Great Sutton Street
London EC1V ODX, UK

www.reaktionbooks.co.uk

First published 2012

Printed and bound in Great Britain
by Bell & Bain, Glasgow

British Library Cataloguing in Publication Data
Bird, Robert, 1969–
    Fyodor Dostoevsky. – (Critical lives)
    1. Dostoyevsky, Fyodor, 1821–1881.
    2. Novelists, Russian – 19th century – Biography.
    I. Title II. Series
    891.7'33-dc23

    ISBN 978 1 86189 900 2

Contents

Mikhail Panov, *Fyodor Dostoevsky*, photographed in 1880.

Introduction: Faces of Dostoevsky

Dostoevsky once asked his friend Stepan Yanovsky, a doctor and amateur phrenologist, to examine his cranium for insight into his character. In the shape of Dostoevsky's skull and in his 'image with tightly clenched lips' Yanovsky discerned a marked similarity to Socrates, reflecting a shared understanding of 'the soul of man'.[1] As with Socrates, contemporary observers were frequently disturbed by the discrepancy between the intellectual authority of Dostoevsky's *daimon* and its sometimes unappealing exterior shell, which hinted at disgraceful secrets concealed within. Sigmund Freud found four distinct faces of Dostoevsky: 'the creative artist, the neurotic, the moralist and the sinner'.[2] As his fame grew in the 1870s, Dostoevsky frequently declined admirers' requests for his photograph, claiming (disingenuously) that he had not sat for a portrait for many years. Dostoevsky's ambivalence suggests that his image presented him with mysteries as well.

No less today the divide between Dostoevsky's compelling creative persona and his troubling human guise continues to be an intellectual, spiritual and even erotic provocation. Readers probe every photograph, every portrait and even posthumous likenesses of Dostoevsky for insight into his powerful, enigmatic works. To see how elusive Dostoevsky's face has proven for artists, just take a glance at the covers of Western editions of his works and of books about him. The only recognizable feature is often the presence of a beard, no matter what shape; it might as well be Rasputin. This was a revolutionary who exchanged cordial notes with the imperial family and their most brutal henchmen, a metaphysician best known for his chatty journalism, an ardent Christian dogged by accusations that he (like Socrates) was corrupting the young.

Some of the stereotypes that have been imposed upon Dostoevsky were no doubt encouraged by aspects of his own life and work. Consider the following description by Comte Eugène-Melchior de Vogüé (1848–1910):

> [Dostoevsky has] the face of a Russian peasant, a true Muscovite *muzhik*: a squashed nose, small eyes flashing beneath high arches of his eyebrows and burning with a flame now gloomy, now tender; a high brow, furrowed by ruts and protrusions, deeply-set temples that seem to be carved out by the blows of a hammer; and all of these features are drawn and distorted, collapsing towards his pained mouth. Never have I seen on the face of a man the expression of such accumulated suffering; it was as if all the trials of his soul and his flesh had left their seal.[3]

This description is obviously over-determined by Dostoevsky's reputation as a Russian nationalist and, in the autobiographical *Notes from the Dead House*, as the first writer to open a window onto the Russian penal colonies. It projects onto the writer the anxious features of such Dostoevskian protagonists as Raskolnikov, Rogozhin and, most of all, Fyodor Pavlovich Karamazov. There is a kind of justice in this; after all, not only did Dostoevsky give the Karamazov patriarch his own Christian name, but he also jotted in his final notebook: 'We are all nihilists [. . .] We are all Fyodor Pavloviches.'[4] No doubt Dostoevsky's face can serve as a mirror for his protagonists, but they are clearly reflected in it only when they turn away from us, their readers. The more we search for Dostoevsky in his works – or for the meaning of his works in his life – the further he and they slip from our grasp.

Dostoevsky's resistance to categorization underscores his fundamental role in articulating the historical turn from a law-based, 'Euclidian' universe to one that could accommodate not only a theory of general relativity, but also the logical quandaries of quantum mechanics. He exempted nothing from radical doubt, making him an unreliable ally for any ideological or religious orthodoxy. The despicable Lebedev in Dostoevsky's *The Idiot* (1868–9) interprets the third horseman of the Apocalypse – who carries 'a pair of scales in his hand' (Revelation 6:5) – as representing the spirit of the modern age, where everything 'is based on the measure and the contract, and everyone is seeking his rightful share'.[5] Dostoevsky designed his apocalyptic fictions as measures of the infinite potentials of humans, for good or for ill, beyond any familiar scale. We his readers have remained slow to measure up, still desiring to contain his works within comfortable truths and ideas, *pro* or *contra*. We still need a more sophisticated, quantum account of the relationship between Dostoevsky's person and his works. Thankfully, since he understood very well just how radical his artistic project was, we can draw guidance in this task from Dostoevsky's own theories of the word and the image.

And so we peer back into Dostoevsky's face. One of the earliest descriptions we have was recorded by Avdotya Panaeva in her diary entry for 15 November 1845, soon after Dostoevsky had suddenly entered the literary scene:

> From the first glance at Dostoevsky you could see that he was a terribly nervous and impressionable young man. He was thin, small and fair-haired, with a sickly facial complexion: small grey eyes shifted cautiously from one object to another, while his pale lips shuddered nervously.[6]

How, Panaeva seems to ask, could this unimpressive physical specimen be the source of such powerful literary images? One of the ways that contemporaries explained his unlikely artistic authority was by reference to what Vogüé called his 'accumulated suffering'. In his description the artist Konstantin Trutovsky, a colleague of Dostoevsky's at engineering school and the author of the first known portrait of the writer (from 1847), projected Dostoevsky's later imprisonment back onto the early years of their friendship:

> At that time Fyodor Mikhailovich was quite slim; his face was pale and grey of hue, his hair fair and fine, his eyes deep-set, but his gaze penetrating and profound [. . .] His movements were somehow awkward and, at the same time, impulsive. His uniform sat clumsily on him, while his pack, hat and rifle seemed like so many chains that he was obliged to bear and which oppressed him.[7]

Note the contrast between Dostoevsky's mechanical bodily movements and the vivacity of his gaze. Dostoevsky's life spirit was so exclusively concentrated in his eyes that 'when he closed his eyes he looked like a corpse', in the words of another memoirist.[8] Thus Dostoevsky becomes himself only on the threshold of death, when he ceases to be a man and has become author. The painful separation between Dostoevsky's outer and inner beings, his proximity to death, forces even sympathetic witnesses to resort to caricature. One witness recorded her impression of Dostoevsky's triumphal speech at the opening of a monument to poet Aleksandr Pushkin in 1880:

> A little man, skinny, grey, fair hair, the colour of his face and of everything was grey. Well, what a figure for a 'Prophet'. And then he grew and grew! He read, and everyone listened, holding their breath. He began quietly and ended as a prophet. His very voice thundered, and he kept growing. A prophet . . .[9]

The dramatic telescoping of scale and perspective again suggests a kind of newspaper caricature, in which the weak body of Dostoevsky is supplanted – one might say, possessed – by the massive corpus of his works.

The constant exchange of energies between Dostoevsky's physical visage and his works is drawn most clearly in the memoir sketch of Varvara Timofeeva, an editor with whom Dostoevsky

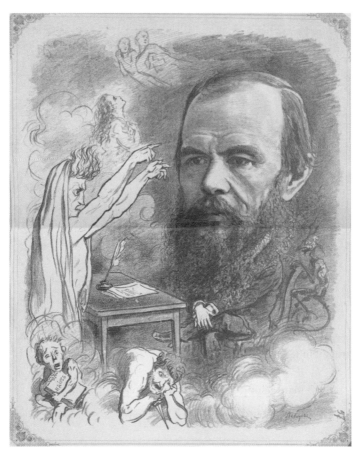

Aleksandr Lebedev, *Caricature of Dostoevsky, the author of Demons*, 1879.

worked on his *Writer's Diary* for 1873. At their first meeting on 20 December 1872 Timofeeva encountered much the same face that had been described by other memoirists:

> This was a very pale man – an earthy, sickly paleness – no longer young, very tired or sickly, with a gloomy, emaciated face that was covered as with a web with some unusually expressive shadows from the tensely restrained flexing of muscles. It was as if every muscle on this face, with its hollow cheeks and broad, elevated brow, was animated by feeling and thought. And these feelings and thoughts irresistibly rushed outwards, where they were restrained by the iron will of this weak yet full-bodied man with broad shoulders, this quiet and gloomy man. He was as if locked up: no movements, not a single gesture, only his thin, bloodless lips shuddered nervously when he spoke. And from the first glance the overall impression reminded me of soldiers, of the 'dishonourably discharged' variety, whom I had frequently seen in my childhood; in general I was reminded of prison, hospital and various 'horrors' from the time of 'serfdom' [. . .] He walked unhurried, with a measured and short step, heavily shifting his weight from foot to foot, as convicts walk in leg-irons.[10]

Not just a prisoner, but a walking prison, enmeshed in a tangle of shadows and shut up by an iron will. However, by March 1873, after Timofeeva has read through several instalments of his *Writer's Diary*, she had discovered another man altogether:

> when, far after midnight, I approached him to say goodbye, he also stood up and, clasping my hand tight, peered into me for a minute with curiosity, as if looking on my face for my impressions from what I had read, as if asking me: what do I think? Have I understood anything?

But I stood before him struck dumb: so astounded was I in these minutes at his own face! Yes, here it is, this is the *true* face of Dostoevsky, just as I had imagined it when reading his novels!

As if illumined by a powerful thought, vividly pale and quite young, with the penetrating gaze of deep, dark eyes, with the expressively silent outline of his thin lips, it breathed with the triumph of its mental force, with proud knowledge of its power . . . This was not a kind or an evil face. It somehow simultaneously attracted and repelled, frightened and captivated . . . And I unconsciously looked upon this face without averting my eyes, as if before me there had opened up a 'tableau vivant' with mysterious content, when you greedily hurry to gather in its meaning, knowing that, just one second more, and all this rare beauty will disappear like a flash of lightning. But in these seconds his face told me more about him than all his articles and novels. This was the face of a *great man*, a historic face [. . .] I walked home, all the way recalling his face and that new inner visage that had been revealed to me.[11]

The difference between the two meetings was not so much that, having begun to work with Dostoevsky, Timofeeva views him differently as a writer or expects some fuller answer from him; quite the opposite: he remains as elusive (and evasive) as ever. The difference is that she is now conscious of Dostoevsky's gaze upon her as his reader and his imposition upon her of severe demands, like the inquisitorial question: 'what are you thinking?' Dostoevsky seeks the physical impression made by his words on her face. It is this new, writerly gaze that transfigures him (from 'face' to 'visage') in Timofeeva's eyes.

Timofeeva's account of Dostoevsky's transfiguration was informed by ideas taken straight out of Dostoevsky's essay 'Apropos the Exhibition', which they were preparing for publication as part of *A Writer's Diary*. The essay, inspired in part by Dostoevsky's experiences when sitting for a portrait by Vasily Perov the previous year, contains some of Dostoevsky's most resolute statements on aesthetics:

> 'One must portray reality as it is', [contemporary artists] say, whereas reality as such does not exist and never has on earth because the essence of things is inaccessible to man; he perceives nature as it is reflected in his ideas, after it has passed through his senses. Accordingly, more scope must be given to the idea, and the ideal should not be feared. A portraitist, for example, seats his subject to paint its portrait; he prepares; he studies the subject carefully. Why does he do that? Because he knows from experience that a person does not always look like himself, and therefore he seeks out 'the principal idea of his physiognomy', that moment when the subject most resembles himself. The portraitist's gift consists in the ability to seek out and capture that moment. And so what is the artist doing here if not trusting first his own idea (the ideal) more than the reality before him? The ideal is also reality, after all, and just as legitimate as immediate reality.[12]

What Dostoevsky is describing – and what so impresses Timofeeva – is a physical exchange of ideas (and ideals) through the face. No separation is ever possible between the idea and the object, and therefore between the artist and his work; they are linked inseparably in the affect they communicate. As poet Charles Olson remarked about the Perov portrait: 'A brand lies upon the temple, and the cheek and mouth are scorched. The mark is there, and the blessing.'[13]

'I never again saw Dostoevsky with this face', Timofeeva says.[14] For all Dostoevsky's Platonizing language about the ideal image, it never appears for more than an instant before it dissipates. Again the thin lips curl, the high brow is caught in shadow, and the silent face recedes back into itself. Dostoevsky knew the mystery of the face. In a study of his manuscripts Konstantin Barsht has shown how Dostoevsky frequently sketched faces as he began to define his characters' identities in words.[15] None of his protagonists – the Underground Man, Raskolnikov, Myshkin, the 'Demons', the Brothers – is ever granted a final illumination of his 'true' face. Even Zosima stinks in the grave. Dostoevsky and his characters exist towards their images, but only as exempla of spirit-made-flesh and flesh-made-spirit; they freeze as images only when they, like Laocoön, become the victims of violence, at the instant of their death. Thus for us they remain caricatures, in the positive sense that, insofar as they are alive, they are constantly subject to metamorphoses that shift the relations of scale and perspective between their outer visages and inward characters, waxing and waning as we engage with them.

This physiognomic instability is one source of the horror that readers registered upon reading Dostoevsky's fictions. As he followed the monthly instalments of *The Brothers Karamazov* in the summer of 1879, Feofil Tolstoy wrote to Dostoevsky's friend Orest Miller:

> It is obvious that Dostoevsky's 'man with flayed skin' in the spirit of Michelangelo warms your gaze. You would hang this anatomical masterpiece, this bloodied flesh, above your desk in order to enjoy its contemplation to the full. I admire it as a conscientious and even anatomically informed work, but I would rather keep it away from my eyes.[16]

The reference is to Michelangelo's portrait of St Bartholomew in *The Last Judgment* in the Sistine Chapel, where the flayed body of the saint holds forth his own skin, the face warped like Salvador Dalí's clocks. This image is proferred as an icon that 'warms'

A detail of Michelangelo's *The Last Judgment* of 1537–41 in the Sistine Chapel, Vatican City, showing St Bartholomew.

Miller's gaze, but for Tolstoy it exposes what should remain hidden from view. Even when he acknowledges his underestimation of the novel (like humble Alyosha before the elder Zosima, he says), Tolstoy reaffirms the parallel to a 'vivisection':

Those who are present at this experiment *in anima vili* see how the muscles ripple, the blood flows in streams, and, most terrible of all, they see themselves reflected in the eyes, this 'mirror of the soul', and in the thoughts of the man whose dissection the author conducts.[17]

One reason, then, that observers seemed so pained by the incommensurability of Dostoevsky's person and his *persona* is that the apocalyptic fantasy of separating body from image pervades his fictions as both a powerful hope and an imminent threat.

'Dostoevsky was too close to me and therefore too unknowable', writes Nikolai Strakhov at the start of his memoir of his sometime friend and confidant.[18] Dostoevsky sought company among those who shared his ideas, but his intimate attention to the physiology of these ideas' incarnation – their *in-flesh-ment* – prevented him from ever belonging to an ideology. Reading Dostoevsky's works, no less than reading his face, requires a constant recalibration between the image and its fleshly presence. No doubt in his attempts to project a healing image onto modern disfigurement there was a great deal of residual Romanticism. Insofar as this desire shaped his social and political views, Dostoevsky always remained a utopian, albeit of a peculiar hue. He was the Romantic who made Romanticism an unsustainable consolation. His fiction was a sustained, radical experiment with literary form that not only engendered forms suitable for, or productive of, modern life: it was, as Jean-Paul Sartre argued, an enticement to freedom.

1

A Noble Vocation

You are to provide concise and clear explanations according to the strict truth to the questions offered here by the imperially sanctioned Investigative Commission:

1) What is your name, patronymic and surname; what is your age; what faith; and have you fulfilled the rites prescribed by religion at the proper time?

Fyodor son of Mikhail Dostoevsky, 27 years of age, Greco-Russian Orthodox. The rites prescribed by religion I have fulfilled at the proper time.

2) Who are your parents, and where are they if they are alive?

My father was a military doctor, Collegiate Councillor Dostoevsky. My mother was of the merchant estate. Both are deceased.

3) Where were you educated, at whose expense and when did you complete your education?

I was educated at the Main College of Engineering at my own expense. I completed my education upon graduating from the officer course of the Main College of Engineering in 1843.

4) Do you serve, and if so, when did you enter the service, what position do you occupy and what rank are you? Also, have you previously been under investigation or on trial, and if so, then for what exactly?

I entered active service upon graduating the highest officer course of the Main College of Engineering in 1843 at the drafting office of the Engineering Department. I resigned in 1844 at the rank of lieutenant. I have never previously been on trial or under investigation.

5) Do you have property or capital, and if not, then what means did you possess for maintaining and housing yourself and your family, if you have one?

At my parents' death, together with my entire remaining family, I inherited an estate numbering 100 souls in Tula province. But in 1845, with the mutual agreement of my relatives, I renounced my portion of the estate for a one-time payout of money. At the present time I have neither property nor capital. I earn my living by literary work, which is how I have existed up to now.

6) With whom have you had close acquaintance and frequent relations?

Completely open relations I have had with no one, apart from my brother, the retired engineer sub-lieutenant Mikhail Dostoevsky . . .[1]

Thus, under interrogation on 8 June 1849, did Fyodor Dostoevsky describe his background and character. He was born on 30 October 1821 (11 November according to the Gregorian calendar) into a family that claimed an ancient noble lineage but had, in recent generations, occupied more humble stations in the regimented society of the Russian Empire. His grandfather was probably a parish priest in Ukraine, possibly in the Eastern Rite Catholic Church. Dostoevsky's father served in Moscow as a doctor at a hospital for the poor – the same hospital where Dostoevsky was born; he gradually ascended the service ranks of society and was granted noble status in 1828. In 1831 the family was able to purchase a country estate: Darovoe (meaning 'given for free') in Tula province, with 100 peasants, including 40 male serfs. In 1832 the estate burned to the ground, leading to a tangle of mortgages and other debts. Legal wrangling over the legacies of his parents and the Kumanins, his aunt and uncle on his mother's side, would provide a constant source of stress during Dostoevsky's life, perhaps even playing a role in the attack that killed him at the age of 59, on 28 January 1881.

Seven children made it into adulthood; Fyodor was the second of four boys. In 1837, soon after their mother's death, Fyodor travelled with his beloved elder brother Mikhail (born 1820) to St Petersburg, where together they prepared for the entrance exams for the Main Engineering School. Mikhail was not accepted, but Fyodor passed his exams brilliantly. A lack of clout prevented him from winning a scholarship and left him reliant on his supportive but impoverished father. He became renowned for his studious ways, earning the monastic nickname 'brother Photius'. He completed his studies in 1843 with the rank of sub-lieutenant and entered the engineering corps in St Petersburg.

By this time the Dostoevsky siblings had also lost their father, who died in June 1839 in circumstances that remain unclear; he either suffered an apoplectic fit or was beaten to death by the peasants on the family estate. It should be said that, regardless of the circumstances, and despite Sigmund Freud's imaginative reconstruction, it would not seem that Fyodor felt at all responsible for his father's death and there is little trace of lasting trauma in his letters and autobiographical notes. Fyodor was left at the mercy of guardians, including the generous Kumanins and the officious Pyotr Karpenin, who became executor of the Dostoevsky estate after marrying Fyodor's sister Varvara in 1840. Though they continued to support him in his studies, his relatives had little inclination to indulge his carefree attitude to money and his fantastic schemes for his future.

From early on Dostoevsky's financial problems were exacerbated by his wholehearted immersion in the imaginary realms opened up by poetry, drama and fiction. He later recalled seeing Friedrich Schiller's *The Robbers* at about the age of ten.[2] In 1835 the family had subscribed to *Biblioteka dlia chteniia* (Library for Reading), which published everything from Pushkin to Balzac and George Sand. On a trip to the Trinity St Sergius Monastery in May 1837 Fyodor and Mikhail regaled their aunt with a 'mass' of poems learned by heart.[3] Years later he would recall a journey made that same month to the capital, together with Mikhail and their father:

My brother and I were rushing into our new life, dreaming about something so frightfully strongly, about everything 'beautiful and lofty' – at that time this word was still fresh and was spoken without irony. And how many such beautiful words there were in circulation at the time! We passionately believed something, and though we both perfectly knew what was needed for the mathematics exam, we dreamed only about poetry and poets. My brother wrote poems, three or so poems every day, even on the road, while I constantly composed in my mind a novel based on Venetian life.[4]

In his first years in St Petersburg Dostoevsky wrote two dramas (*Mary Stuart* and *Boris Godunov*, both lost) and tried his hand at translating his favourite French authors, Eugène Sue (1804–1857) and Honoré de Balzac (1799–1850); his translation of Balzac's *Eugénie Grandet* (1833) was published in a journal in 1844. He confessed to his brother that he was completing a novel 'the length of *Eugénie Grandet*'.[5] Already at this time Dostoevsky conceived of fiction as a powerful force for personal and social liberation, if also a source of risk.

Tired of parades and ceremonial displays before the emperor, in August 1844 Dostoevsky resigned his commission. The lack of a constant income led Dostoevsky to request that he be paid his inheritance in a lump sum of 500 roubles, with 500 more to be paid in instalments. His relatives were shocked at how cheaply he rated his inheritance, but they acceded to his request; it was advantageous to them. There are competing accounts of the circumstances that led to Dostoevsky's resignation from the engineering corps. There was at the time a rumour that he was asked to resign when the emperor noticed that a draft Dostoevsky made for a fortress lacked a front gate. This rumour not only fed on Dostoevsky's absent-mindedness but on his emotional insularity. It is the first hint of the claustrophobic images of imprisonment that soon came to pervade Dostoevsky's fictions, halfway between Piranesi and Escher.

Having selected the new vocation of the professional writer, for the rest of his life Dostoevsky would try to make it compensate for his compromised birthright.[6] Writing in 1877 to a fourteen-year-old, Dostoevsky recalled that he had been intent on a literary career from the age of sixteen: 'in my soul there was a kind of flame in which I believed, though I was not too concerned with what would come of it'.[7] At the same time, Dostoevsky stressed,

> *my* infatuation [with a literary career] did not distract me at all from holding a realistic view of life, and though I was a poet, not an engineer, I was always one of the top students at the engineering school until the very last year; then I served, and

though I knew that sooner or later I would leave the service, *for the while* I did not see anything in *my social* occupations that was too irreconcilably hostile to my future; on the contrary, I firmly believed that the future still would be mine and that I *alone* was its master.[8]

The confidence granted by his poetic vocation gave him the means for dealing with such traumas as the death of his parents. Reflecting upon it, Dostoevsky wrote to his brother in 1839:

My soul is beyond my former tempestuous impulses. It is entirely serene, like the heart of a man who conceals a profound mystery. Man is a mystery. One has to solve it, and if you spend all your life solving it you won't be able to say that you've wasted your time. I am occupied with this mystery because I want to be a man [. . .] I think there is no ascetic holier than the poet. How can one commit one's ecstasy to paper? The soul always conceals more than it can express in words, colours or sounds.[9]

From his earliest surviving letters on, Dostoevsky always signed with his full name (F. Dostoevsky or Fyodor Dostoevsky), even when writing to his family and closest friends.[10] He was fashioning himself as an author.

Though his impudence and inconstancy strained his relations with family and colleagues, Dostoevsky appears almost to have cultivated these stresses as major sources of his fiction, most directly of the novel *Poor Folk*, the first draft of which he completed about a year after resigning his commission. The novel, like almost all of Dostoevsky's writing, is a study of the forces that constrain human freedom, both exterior forces such as money and power, and interior ones like illness and sexual desire. Moreover Dostoevsky immediately set about questioning the very distinction between the two realms, showing how subjective experience becomes objectified

Konstantin Trutovsky, *Portrait of Fyodor Dostoevsky*, 1847.

in material objects of desire and fear, and vice versa. However, like most of Dostoevsky's fiction, *Poor Folk* also revealed his belief in the power of fiction to redeem the world by manifesting an imaginative realm in which freedom is – or, at least, can be – sovereign.

Poor Folk is an epistolary novel chronicling the doomed love of the pathetic Makar Devushkin for his beloved Varvara. Dostoevsky is equally attentive to the details of material life, and the media by which this life is informed by characters' desires and fantasies, especially literature (from the dubious 'Italian Passions' to Pushkin and Gogol) and letter-writing. He comes to know himself through these imaginary portraits: 'For I feel exactly the same thing, in precisely the same way as in the book, and I've sometimes found myself in exactly the same situations.'[11] However, he also finds himself imprisoned in the imaginary realm. Varvara ends up making a pragmatic marriage to the merchant Bykov, writing to Makar: 'I leave you your book, my tambour, and an unfinished letter; when you look at these lines I began to write you can read with your thoughts anything you would have liked to hear or read from me, everything that I could have written to you.'[12] Makar is left to work on his literary style: 'I write only in order to write, only to write to you as much as possible.'[13]

Makar was the first of many protagonists in Dostoevsky's fiction who fail to escape the imaginary. The novel's mixed reception revealed that, as an author, Dostoevsky was also hermetically sealed in his own imagination. One witty critic complained:

The novel has no form and is based completely on details so tiringly monotonous that it invokes a tedium the likes of which we have never experienced before. The details in the novel are like a meal in which instead of soup one is given sugar bon-bons, and instead of beef, sauce, stew and dessert – sugar bon-bons. It might be sweet, it might be useful, but only in the sense in which sweetshop apprentices are allowed to gorge themselves in order to inspire disgust for sugary sweets.[14]

Others found the sentimentalism quite powerful. Upon reading *Poor Folk* in manuscript, Nikolai Nekrasov (1821–1877), a leading poet and publisher of the day, rushed to meet the author in the middle of the night – a Petersburg white night in which the sun dips just below the horizon for a fleeting couple of hours. His enthusiasm was shared by Vissarion Belinsky (1811–1848), the leading critic and trend-setter. The novel was published in Nekrasov's almanac in 1846 and as a separate edition in 1847. By that time the adulation of Nekrasov and Belinsky had already been diluted by their dismay at Dostoevsky's puzzling follow-up novel *The Double*, which was published in Andrei Kraevsky's journal *Otechestvennye zapiski* (Notes of the Fatherland) in February 1846; but this consternation was hopefully dismissed. The future of Russian literature – and with it, to a large degree, of Russian civil society – seemed to rest with his talented, socially committed pen. By 1848 Dostoevsky was on course to achieve the cultural legitimacy and financial independence he so craved.

The European revolutions of 1848 found Russia in a state of severe cultural depression, fostered by the paranoid regime of Emperor Nicholas I. Nicholas had acceded to power in the midst of the Decembrist revolt of 1825, led by educated officers hankering for constitutional reform. After suppressing the revolt, Nicholas prohibited many forms of public discourse and instituted vigilant censorship over the rest. Philosophy as a subject was banned at the universities. When Pyotr Chaadaev (1794–1856) sneaked his 'First Philosophical Letter' past the censors in 1836, he was declared mad and kept under house arrest.

Chaadaev's argument in this letter was that Russia was a blank space without any history or other redeeming features:

At first brutal barbarism, then crude superstition, then cruel and humiliating foreign domination, the spirit of which was later inherited by our national rulers – such is the sad history of our youth. We had none of that exuberant activity, of the fervent turmoil of the moral forces of nations [. . .] There are no charming remembrances, no graceful images in the people's memory; our national tradition is devoid of any powerful teaching.[15]

Chaadaev's argument struck at the heart of both traditional Russian culture, centred on Orthodox Christianity, and of the modernizing and Europeanizing project that Peter the Great had embarked upon at the turn of the eighteenth century. As part of Peter's plan, St Petersburg was founded in 1703 on a dank northern estuary in order to project Russian power out over the seas. As the city settled into the Russian imaginary its canals filled with ink; an imaginative construct, imperial Petersburg was equal parts fantasy and nightmare, utopia and abyss. The traumas of modernization and the constraints on their open public discussion made imaginative art and literature a means not only of measuring historical change, but also of modulating it for educated individuals. By the late eighteenth century a vibrant poetry and, increasingly, fiction had arisen and had come to perform many of the functions accorded to philosophy and political theory in the contemporary European societies on which Russian was modelling itself. Aleksandr Pushkin (1799–1837) and Nikolai Gogol (1809–1851) were two of the first individuals who were able to exist as professional writers. Moreover artistic and literary criticism became unusually important as a venue for public discourse. Critic Vissarion Belinsky, in particular, became a major conduit for philosophical idealism and political radicalism. This was the milieu into which Dostoevsky gained entry with his *Poor Folk*.

Dostoevsky's letter to his brother Mikhail of 24 March 1845 shows how intently he plotted his entrance onto the stage of

Russian literature. Fearing that censors and editors would delay *Poor Folk*, Dostoevsky considered publishing it himself:

> To publish oneself means to thrust one's chest forwards, and if the work is good, it will not only hold its own, but will redeem me from subjection to debt and give me food.
> And now about food! You know, brother, that in this respect I am left to my own powers. But come what may, however dire my circumstances, I have pledged to bear up and not take commissions. Commissions will crush and destroy everything. I want each of my works to be distinctly good. Look at Pushkin and Gogol. They didn't write much, but monuments await both. And now Gogol gets 1,000 roubles in silver for each signature [about twenty pages], while Pushkin, as you know, sold each line for ten roubles. But then their glory was paid for by years of penury and starvation [. . .] Raphael painted for years, refining and honing his works, and created miracles; gods were created by his hands.[16]

Dostoevsky's ambition became legend. One persistent rumour (which resurfaced as late as the 1870s) had Dostoevsky demanding that *Poor Folk* be published in an unusual typeface and with a decorative border around the page. His credo, expressed in a letter to Mikhail from 26 November 1846, was to attain

> an independent position [. . .] work for Holy Art, sacred work, pure, in the simplicity of my heart which has never before shuddered and moved as it does now before all the new images which are being created in my soul. Brother, I am being reborn not only morally, but also physically.[17]

Gogol and Raphael, modern St Petersburg and Renaissance Rome, authorial hubris and sacred purity: from the very beginning

Dostoevsky was caught in the tension between the nobility of his aims and the limitations of his immediate position.

The tension is captured in the word *fantaziia*, which for Dostoevsky meant both liberating imagination and debilitating illusion. He consistently defined his own artistic method as 'fantastic realism', which looks beyond surface reality to the forces that animate human action. After embarking on his vocation Dostoevsky quickly became aware of the dangers attending such a complete immersion in fiction, writing to his brother at the beginning of 1847:

> You see, the more we have of spirit and inner content, the better our corner [of the world] and our life. Of course, it is terrifying to think of the dissonance, the imbalance, which society represents for us. The *outer* must be balanced with the *inner*. Otherwise, in the absence of outer phenomena, the inner will attain dangerous ascendancy. Nerves and imagination [*fantaziia*] will take up too much space in one's being.[18]

It was increasingly obvious to him, however, that he was far from balanced:

> I recall that you once told me that my behaviour with you excludes mutual equality. My beloved. This was utterly unjust. But I have such a mean, repulsive character [. . .] My nerves are not obeying me at these moments. I am ridiculous and disgusting, and therefore always suffer from unjust opinions about me. They say I am stale and heartless [. . .] But soon you will read *Netochka Nezvanova*. This will be a confession, like *Golyadkin*, although in another tone and kind. [. . .] My pen is ruled by a spring of inspiration that flows straight from my soul.[19]

Throughout his first works, then, Dostoevsky wrote in order to heal the perceived split between private and public, personal and artistic selves, learning to write sincerely but with objective effect.

The Double dramatizes this divided consciousness in three distinct realms: the city, the modern mind and the work of fiction. Created as the seat of a new government, ruled by the new hierarchy of service ranks and social prestige, St Petersburg is a city of illusions and, as Dostoevsky's Underground Man later says, the 'most abstract and premeditated city in the whole world'.[20] Amid these surroundings Mr Golyadkin, absorbed in his own mirror-image and the 'noble sum' of his savings, tries to project the persona of a successful modern bureaucrat.[21] He hires a carriage, dresses his servant in livery and sets off to impress, opening the windows wide despite the winter chill. Unfortunately he runs into his boss and is forced to 'pretend that it is not me, but someone else who looks strikingly similar to me'.[22] Gradually this more suave and successful image materializes as Mr Golyadkin Jr, who displaces Mr Golyadkin Sr at work and in the affections of the coveted Klara. Unable to gain recognition for what he wants to be, Mr Golyadkin ceases to be recognized at all and comes 'to doubt his own existence'.[23] He is erased from the city, just as the city seems to be on the verge of being erased from history.

This raises a clear problem for Dostoevsky's own work: how can he project an image that will, instead of proliferating the continued fragmentation of social and psychological reality, instead of adding yet another layer of virtuality and caprice to a world that has lost its moorings, help to heal the divide? How can his fictions avoid the fate of self-erasure that threatens his dreamy, imaginative characters? In the eyes of earnest critics, the lack of a formal resolution to *The Double* and its follow-up stories 'Mr Prokharchin' and 'The Landlady' compromised their social function. Belinsky noted 'the inability of a talent too richly endowed with capabilities to determine the reasonable measure and limits for the artistic development of his conception'.[24] In retrospect we can see that Dostoevsky was enacting in his fiction a drama of disintegration analogous to those he found in the world. Nonetheless, Dostoevsky suffered a severe crisis of confidence, consoling himself with unlikely hopes:

> About *Golyadkin* I hear murmurings (from many) of such frightful rumours. Some say that this work is a *miracle* and has been misunderstood. That it has a frightful role to play in the future, that if I'd only written *Golyadkin* that it would be enough, and that for some it is more interesting that the interest of Dumas. Look how my pride has burst out. But, brother! How nice it is to be understood. Brother, for what do you love me so! – I will try to embrace you soon. We will love each other passionately.[25]

Thus Dostoevsky cycled endlessly from despair to exalted hope, so reliant on his ambitions that the prospect of success seemed 'frightful'.

Dostoevsky's third major work, *White Nights*, both dramatizes its author's dilemma and points the way to some kind of resolution. The protagonist is similar to Mr Golyadkin in significant respects. He circulates around Petersburg, especially on Nevsky Prospect, as a *flâneur* – a word and notion that Dostoevsky introduced into the Russian language. He is cut off from the country and, by extension, from traditional forms of life. Nature in Petersburg reminds him of a sickly girl who evokes pity. He is also obsessed with external images: he states that he knows the entire city population because he has 'made a very thorough study of their physiognomies', and his mood responds to what he observes: 'I am happy when they are happy, and I am sad when they are overcast with care.'[26] He has similarly evocative encounters with buildings:

I shall never forget the incident with a pretty little house of a pale pink hue. It was such a dear little house; it always welcomed me with such a friendly smile, and it looked upon its clumsy neighbours with such an air of condescension, that my heart leaped with joy every time I passed it. But when I happened to walk along the street only a week ago and looked up at my friend, I was welcomed with a most plaintive cry, 'They are going to paint me yellow!' Fiends! Savages! They spared nothing, neither cornices, nor columns, and my poor friend turned as yellow as a canary. I nearly had an attack of jaundice myself, and even to this day I have not been able to screw up my courage to go and see my mutilated friend, painted in the national colour of the Celestial Empire![27]

We might diagnose this dreamer's condition as one of imaginative sympathy; like Mr Golyadkin, he mimics his surroundings and creates a kind of alternative reality for himself, ending up enclosed within the four walls of his room, with its cobwebs in the corners, which represents his solipsistic enclosure within his own cranium. And yet *White Nights* is ultimately a bright and hopeful hymn to the power of the imagination. Joseph Frank concludes that here 'The power of imagination is glorified in the very act of seeming to pass censure upon its effects.'[28]

One day our unnamed protagonist sees a girl being pursued by a would-be assailant and instantly falls in love with her:

if only you knew how many times I've fallen in love like that! [. . .] With no one, of course. Just my ideal, with the woman I see in my dreams. I make up all sorts of romances [*romany*] in my dreams.[29]

The girl, named Nastya, responds in kind, holding back a secret until their next meeting so that 'at least from a distance it will seem more like a romance [*roman*]'.[30] The key word in both comments is *roman*, which is also the word for novel. There are hints of the dangers involved in living out a novel like this. He asks Nastya:

'Listen, do you want to know what kind of person I am?'
'Well, yes, yes!'
'In the strictest meaning of the word?'
'Yes, in the strictest meaning of the word!'
'Very well, I'm a character [*tip*].'[31]

Though his attraction to Nastya is deeply erotic, he defines the dreamer – and thus himself also – as 'a sort of creature of the neuter gender', hinting at his despair that his desire and dreams will never take flesh and blood. Nastya tells him he speaks as if he were reading from a book', which he misunderstands to mean that he speaks beautifully, like the spirit of Solomon after a thousand-year captivity.[32] But his over-fertile imagination is mired in a crisis of authenticity. He likens the act of dreaming within one's four walls to 'forging paper money', or 'writing atrocious poetry' that one tries to put over as the work of one's deceased friend.[33] In fact the problem is writing, pure and simple. As one obsessive writer in *The Idiot* would later say, 'I won't achieve syntax before I die.'[34]

By contrast with Mr Golyadkin, however, this time the dreamer's imagination produces a healing image that can at least cushion the pain of modern existence. The dreamer tells a story of how a tired man with 'weak nerves and a morbidly excited imagination' is ennobled by 'the farewell ray of the setting sun [which] flashed so gaily across his vision and called forth a whole swarm of impressions from his glowing heart'.[35] This is an avowedly romantic picture; the protagonist explicitly attributes the figure of the Goddess of Fancy (or Fantasy) to the early Romantic poet Vasily Zhukovsky (1783–1852). Yet even when this 'castle in the air comes crumbling noiselessly around him, without a sound, and it vanishes like a dream, without leaving a trace', the dreamer is still inspired by its memory:

> Silence reigns in the little room; solitude and a feeling of indolence caress his imagination [. . .] His imagination is once more tuned up, excited, and suddenly a new world, a new fascinating life, once more sparkles before him in a sparkling vision [. . .] Look at those magical phantoms which – so enchantingly, so capriciously, so boundlessly and so vastly – are composed before him in so magical and animated a picture, a picture in which, needless to say, he himself, our dreamer, in his own precious person, occupies the foregound as the protagonist! Look at what diverse adventures, what an infinite swarm of ecstatic dreams![36]

The dreamer is 'the artist of his own life, which he re-creates in himself to suit whatever new fancy he pleases. And how easily, how naturally, is this imaginary, fantastic world created! As though it were not a phantom at all!'[37] Even in prison-like St Petersburg, which constrains the individual's every move in predetermined channels and ruts, freedom remains possible, if only for a fleeting instant, as a matter of illumination.

Life, Dostoevsky was coming to believe, is the informing of reality with the imagination and memory. One cannot be true to real life, he suggests, without considering the effects of the imaginary. Even if images fail to have an impact, our memory of the image, the ideal, remains as a pledge of its realization in the future. The protagonist's act of telling the story to Nastya reconciles him to himself and allows him to promise that 'I shall never again think so ill of myself . . . I shall never again accuse myself of committing a crime and a sin.'[38] Still, the protagonist's confession elicits only pity from Nastya, and he immediately retreats into self-recriminations for his inability to conjure up anything more than the ashes of his failed dreams – perhaps precisely because he continues to speak at Nastya, rather than with her, and to treat her as a listener, but never as a speaker in her own right. We are here already on the doorstep of the Underground.

The dream does, however, prompt Nastya to tell the story of how she has been virtually imprisoned by her grandmother, who (as in Pushkin's 'The Queen of Spades') makes Nastya read books out loud to her. Nastya fell in love with their lodger, only to be abandoned by him when he moved to Moscow for a year. Now he is back in St Petersburg and she is eagerly anticipating the resumption of their affair.

'I had never expected such a denouement', our protagonist confesses.[39] He dictates to her a letter by which she can safely request clarity, but when he sees she has already written her own letter they sing out an aria from Rossini's *The Barber of Seville* in unison: 'Rosina!'[40] They inhabit the same fictional space, which allows for communication and, eventually, action, though it appears to rule out physical love. Awaiting his response, she confesses to doubts that 'perhaps my love for [the lodger] was nothing but a deception of feeling, of imagination', but still she is determined to remain true to her image of him, and sure enough he returns to claim her.[41] She writes a farewell letter to the dreamer:

Thank you, yes! thank you for that love. For it remains imprinted in my memory like a sweet dream one remembers a long time after awakening [. . .] If you forgive me, I promise you that the memory of you will always be elevated within me with an eternal, grateful feeling for you, which will never be erased from my heart . . . I shall treasure this memory, I'll be true to it and will not betray my heart.[42]

The dreamer is left with nothing, but perhaps he has the key to freedom in his memory: 'My God! An entire minute of bliss? Is that so little even for the whole of a man's life?'[43]

Already in his earliest works Dostoevsky deployed a riotous idiom that drew philosophical terminology and urban slang into a veritable whirlpool of language. His humour frequently verging upon hysteria, Dostoevsky seems at times almost in the thrall of his own verbal inventiveness, boasting about the neologisms (many derived from slang) he introduced to the Russian language. His characters are drawn in their speech no less than in their physical and intellectual profiles. Each is defined by his or her struggle to 'achieve syntax' without compromising their individuality.

As an artist Dostoevsky has sometimes been accused of carelessness and inconsistency, especially when compared to the regal calm of Tolstoy and the majestic grace of Turgenev. (He frequently felt oppressed by the comparison to his noble competitors.) Nonetheless, from his earliest writings Dostoevsky deployed a consistent and precise terminology to mark his central concerns, including the crucial trio of terms: face/person (*litso*), fantasy/imagination (*fantaziia*) and impressions (*vpechatlenie*). In 1874, at the beginning of his work on *The Adolescent*, Dostoevsky provided a precise statement of his method:

> In order to write a novel one must first secure *one* or *several* powerful impressions that the author's heart has really experienced. *This is the task of the poet.* Out of this impression develops a theme, a plan, a measured whole [*stroinoe tseloe*]. *This is the task of the artist*, although the artist and poet help each other [. . .] in both cases.[44]

As Konstantin Barsht points out, one senses Dostoevsky's architectural training in his emphasis on *planning* and *measure* as the tasks of the artist: 'The oblong page of a "note book" was for Dostoevsky

a model of the four-dimensional "chronotope" of the future work.'[45]
Only through artistry can the work create effects in the physical
world commensurate to the imaginary ('poetic') conception.

The story 'Mr Prokharchin' in particular illustrates how
Dostoevsky was thinking about fictional form as a physical body
capable of creating effects in the world beyond the projection
of a spectral healing image. One of the literary fashions was for
'physiological sketches', which were documentary essays analysing
prominent types of city life. Dostoevsky was obviously eager to
absorb impressions from contemporary reality, but he refused to
stop at their mere documentation. Instead he focused on the states
of mind of his world's denizens and experimented with literary
forms capable of capturing them. In both senses he thought
physiologically. This is not to say that he was always successful.
Of his 'Mr Prokharchin', Dostoevsky wrote to his brother on 17
September 1846: 'Prokharchin is horribly disfigured in a sensitive
place. Everything vivid has disappeared. There remains only the
skeleton.'[46]

Despite his success Dostoevsky's correspondence continued
to consist largely of requests for money: promises to repay money
already borrowed and increasingly delusional get-rich-quick
schemes in which he tried to involve his brothers, relatives and
friends. It is beyond doubt that he was usually broke but, given
his literary earnings and the generosity of those around him, one
has to wonder what he did with the sums he earned. Some of his
friends suggested that he was unreasonably generous and easily
taken advantage of. Such a view might receive confirmation from
the unthinking charity of characters in his novels, from Ivan
Petrovich in *The Insulted and the Injured* to Raskolnikov in *Crime
and Punishment*. As in so many cases, however, it's difficult to
know whether Dostoevsky was describing himself or whether his
readers have simply extrapolated about him from his creations.
More plausible is the link between Dostoevsky's constant financial

difficulties and the nervous complaint from which he suffered and which contributed to his overexcited state of mind, which is described by contemporaries as impressionability and hyperbolism. He later recalled that in 1847–9 he had suffered from an illness of the digestive tract that at times caused 'moral and emotional distress': 'A man [with this illness] is infected by infinite mistrust and ends up imagining himself sick with all possible sicknesses.'[47] There is also the curious postscript to his letter to Mikhail from 16 November 1845 which suggests that, at the crest of his initial fame, Dostoevsky was lavishing money on prostitutes:

> All the Minushkas, Klarushkas and Mariannas have become impossibly pretty. The other day Turgenev and Belinsky took me to task for my disorderly life. These gentlemen don't even realize how much they love me [. . .] My debts remain at their previous level.[48]

By the time of his arrest Dostoevsky was comparing his struggle with creditors to Laocoön's with the serpents.[49]

The analogy to Laocoön is equally apt for Dostoevsky's struggles to develop fictional forms capable of dealing with modernity without succumbing to its hazards. Dostoevsky's most important early works – *Poor Folk*, *The Double* and *White Nights* – all lament the disfigurement of society and of the individual psyche under the pressures of modern life. The main characters seek a healing image, most often in young women they see but can never possess either as body or as image. *Poor Folk* and *White Nights* provide pledges of a healing image that can be retained in memory, but there appears to be no antidote for the abandonment, disfigurement and even imprisonment that the fleeting image leaves in its wake. The aesthetic creed that emerges in Dostoevsky's early writings recognizes the origin of artistic images in the imagination but insists on the need for them to receive full incarnation in physical reality. Thus the artist, for Dostoevsky, ideally serves as a medium for the communication of socially constructive affect. How precisely to live up to this role was a question that tortured Dostoevsky throughout his life.

Dostoevsky was never really able to reclaim the figure of a nobleman, even when his material affairs finally improved in the last years of his life. Moreover, he was never even able to render a single truly noble figure in his fiction, dominated as it was by the carnal landowners Valkovsky and Versilov, the idiot prince Myshkin and the demonic imposter Stavrogin. His archly gothic imagination was attracted to the extremes of beauty and disfiguration, of exhilaration and despair, which scarred the modern cityscape. Emerging as a writer out of a world of archaic beliefs and hierarchies, Dostoevsky fashioned himself as the chronicler of what would come next.

2

Ten Years of Silence

On the morning of 22 December 1849 21 young men were led out
to the parade grounds of the St Simeon Regiment in St Petersburg
to learn their sentence and submit to their punishment. They were
all members of a revolutionary cell which, the authorities alleged,
had gradually turned from naive reverie to an active conspiracy to
subvert the government of Tsar Nicholas I. In retribution for the
white nights of early summer, winter days in St Petersburg end
almost before they begin. Emerging onto the parade ground under
the leaden sky, the convicts were stunned into morbid silence by
a sentence of death pronounced on each and every one. They were
given a crucifix to kiss, in accordance with Orthodox custom. As
officers (like all educated men in this militarized society), they
underwent a ritual expulsion from the army, with swords snapped
over their heads. As if for baptism, they were dressed in virgin-
white robes. Heavy with guilt and in joyless surroundings, three
by three, the convicts began the trudge up to their death.

From the second group, Dostoevsky watched as the first three-
some were tied to wooden poles, which stood at an annoyingly
untidy slant. He remembered his beloved brother Mikhail and his
young family. Realizing that he had but seconds to live, he bitterly
regretted that he could not glimpse anything hopeful or comforting.
He cast his eyes to the skies and wondered whether prayer would
not be counted against him. He looked before him as the drums
beat out the command . . .

Dostoevsky was arrested in the dawn hours of 23 April 1849, after returning late from visiting friends. According to a later notation he became vaguely aware of the presence of 'suspicious and unusual people' in his room and fought off his slumber, only to awaken into a nightmare that would last ten years.[1] He was taken to police headquarters, where he encountered some of the dozens of young men taken in that morning. It was St George's Day, which until the sixteenth century had marked a brief period of freedom in Russia when peasants had been free to change their master. One of Dostoevsky's friends noted the irony when they met in the corridors of the police station.

The group with which Dostoevsky had become mixed up in early 1847 was known as the Petrashevtsy, after the man who hosted their Friday evening conversations. Mikhail Butashevich-Petrashevsky (1821–1866) collected banned books, particularly those of European socialists, and encouraged criticism of the social order in Russia, particularly the persistence of serfdom. If nothing else the circle was an effective school for future Russian thinkers; apart from Dostoevsky the Petrashevtsy included the philosopher Nikolai Danilevsky (1822–1885), the satirist Mikhail Saltykov-Shchedrin (1826–1889), the poet Aleksei Pleshcheev (1825–1893) and several other notable talents.

Dostoevsky's arrest had been instigated by his reading of correspondence between Nikolai Gogol and Vissarion Belinsky in which the critic had excoriated the writer for his declarations of fidelity to the Orthodox Church, which Belinsky associated with the repressive autocracy. In the course of long interrogations Dostoevsky insisted that he read the incriminating letters out of pure interest, having been an acolyte of Gogol's art and a protégé of Belinsky's theories, and that 'he did not agree with a single one of the exaggerations found in this article'.[2] In their search of Dostoevsky's flat the police also confiscated two banned books, a socialist tract by Eugène Sue and a critique of religion by P. J. Proudhon, thereby confirming their suspicion that Dostoevsky was trafficking in sedition. In his letter to Gogol, Belinsky had written:

> The most vital national problems in Russia today are the abolition of serfdom and corporal punishment and the strictest possible observance of at least those laws that already exist [. . .] Such are the problems that prey on the mind of Russia in her apathetic slumber! And at such a time a great writer, whose astonishingly artistic and deeply truthful works have so powerfully contributed toward Russia's awareness of herself, enabling her as they did to take a look at herself as though in a mirror – publishes a book in which he teaches the barbarian landowner to make still greater profits out of the peasants and to abuse them still more in the name of Christ and the Church [. . .] Had you really been inspired by the truth of Christ and not by the teaching of the devil you would certainly have written something entirely different in your new book. You would have told the landowner that since his peasants are his brethren in Christ, and since a brother cannot be a slave to his brother, he should either give them their freedom or, at least, allow them to enjoy the fruits of their own labor to their greatest possible benefit, realizing, as he does, in the depths of his own conscience, the false relationship in which he stands toward them.[3]

Though directed wholly at a single writer, after the turmoil of 1848 such rhetoric constituted sedition against the state. However harsh it seems today, no one expressed surprise at the severity of the sanction when Dostoevsky was arrested and sentenced to death for disseminating it.

It remains entirely possible that Dostoevsky got off lightly. His lifelong friend Apollon Maikov (1821–1897), arrested as an associate of the plotters but soon released, recalled Dostoevsky trying to recruit him for a sub-group led by Nikolai Speshnyov

(1821–1882) which had procured a printing press and was intent on raising the stakes of their sedition. He described Dostoevsky's visit at the start of 1849: 'sitting like the dying Socrates before his friends, in a night shirt with an unbuttoned front, [he] summoned all his grandiloquence to demonstrate the sacred nature of this cause, our obligation to save the fatherland, etc.'[4] Later in life Dostoevsky also hinted that the authorities had missed the real plot. However, his other close friend Yanovsky suggested that these rumours stemmed from Dostoevsky's usual hyperbolism and, perhaps, his attempts to curry favour with the even more radicalized youth of the 1870s, especially after he had alienated them with the unsympathetic portrait of revolutionary plotters in *Demons*.

The thinker with the greatest influence on the Petrashevtsy was Charles Fourier (1772–1837), whose utopian version of socialism featured the destruction of traditional human dwellings and the construction of barracks-like phalansteries, around which life could be organized rationally. To his inquisitors, Dostoevsky remarked,

As far as we – Russia, Petersburg – are concerned, it's enough to walk twenty paces along the street to become convinced that on our soil Fourierism can exist only in the uncut pages of a book or in a soft, gentle and dreamy soul, but in no other form than that of an idyll or a verse poem in 24 cantos.[5]

In his interrogations and deposition he held true to the view that, as a writer of fiction, he worked outside conventional ideological categories:

My view was radically opposed to that of Belinsky. I reproached him for trying to give literature a partisan and unnatural task by lowering it to an account of, so to speak, *newspaper facts* or scandalous events [. . .]

In general I am not a talkative person and do not like to speak loudly wherever there are people I do not know. My mindset and I myself am known only to a very few friends. I avoid major disputes and prefer to yield in order to be left in peace. But I was challenged to take part in this literary dispute, the point of which, from my point of view, was that art has no need of tendency [*napravlenie*], that art is an end in itself, that an author need only concern himself with artistic quality [*khudozhestvennost'*] and the idea will come of its own accord, for it is an essential condition of artistic quality. In a word, *it is obvious that this approach* [*napravlenie*] *is diametrically opposite to that of a newspaper and a fire brigade.*[6]

Dostoevsky brazenly declared to his interrogators that the government must show more trust of writers and pardon his apparent crimes in recognition of his service to society:

I was sad that the vocation of the writer has been diminished in our time by some dark suspicion and that the censors view a writer, before he's even written anything, as a kind of natural enemy of the government and deal with his manuscript with obvious prejudice [. . .] As if by hiding vice and the dark side of life you will hide from the reader that vice and the dark side of life exist in the world. No, the author will not hide this dark side by systematically concealing it from the reader, but will only suspect himself of insincerity and untruthfulness. Can you paint with only bright colours? How will the bright side of the painting be visible without the dark, can there be a painting without light and shadow together? We know about light only because shadow exists.[7]

Without a single expression of remorse or self-justifying excuse, in his interrogations the prisoner Dostoevsky forthrightly portrayed himself as a martyr in the name of literature: 'Who will formulate new ideas so that the people can understand them if not literature! . . . Without literature society cannot exist, and I saw that literature was dying.'[8] In short, Dostoevsky remarks, 'literature needs no tendency, art is a goal in itself, the artist should simply concern himself with artistry and the idea will come of its own accord, for it is a necessary condition of artistry'.[9]

As elsewhere in his life, it would seem that Dostoevsky kept his true commitments secret. In his deposition to the prosecuting authorities he expanded on this theme:

> In essence I still do not know what I am being accused of [. . .] Who has seen into my soul? Who determined the degree of betrayal, harm and rebellion of which I am accused? [. . .] I don't recall ever opening up *in full, as I really am*, at Petrashevsky's [. . .] no denunciation will ever make me other than I really am. [. . .] I am accused of reading the article 'Belinsky's Correspondence with Gogol' at one of Petrashevsky's evenings. Yes, I read it, but can the person who has denounced me say which of the two correspondents I preferred?[10]

What emerges from these remarkable documents is the image of a man striving to remain true to his artistic vocation in the face of crushing physical and psychological blows. He speaks openly without implicating a single one of his acquaintances. His physical existence is of less concern to him than his dignity as a writer and an intellectual, on which he still, against the odds, places unreasonable hopes.

At the time of his arrest Dostoevsky was in the process of writing a novel, *Netochka Nezvanova*, a first-person narrative of a young girl from a downtrodden family. The third instalment appeared in *Otechestvennye zapiski* after Dostoevsky's arrest, without the author's name. By the time of the execution on 22 December Dostoevsky had spent exactly eight months in the fortress, during which time he continued to write, completing the story 'A Children's Tale', published in 1857 (again, without Dostoevsky's name) as 'The Little Hero'. The narrator, an unnamed eleven-year-old boy, tells of his summer at a relative's estate, where he was surrounded by beautiful women engaged in erotic play. The idyll sours when the boy falls in love with the mysterious Mme M. and ends up in embarrassing situations, unable to understand or control this new feeling:

> To be honest, I myself was unable to name what I was so afraid of; however I was afraid of something and trembled like a leaf in fear of this *something* being revealed. The only thing I did not know until this minute was what it was: is it any good or not, is it healthy or shameful, laudable or not? Now, in torments and violent grief, I realized that it was *ridiculous* and *disgraceful*![11]

Given the circumstances in which Dostoevsky found himself, the story might seem a mere diversion, perhaps an escape into memories of idyllic summers spent at his parents' estate. However it is worth reading closely into the agitation felt by the boy at his awakening:

> Hardly catching my breath, resting my elbows on the grass, I looked unconsciously and motionlessly before myself, at the surrounding hills striped with rows of grain; at the river which snaked around them and flowed far into the distance, as far as the eye could see, between new hills and villages which flashed like points of light across the entire illuminated distance; at the blue, hardly-visible woods, as if smoking at the edge of the red-hot sky; and some sweet peace, as if inspired by the solemn silence of the picture, gradually tamed my indignant heart. I felt easier, and I breathed freer . . . But my entire soul suffered

silently and sweetly, as if with a premonition of something, as if a presentiment of something. My frightened heart, trembling slightly from anticipation, was shyly and joyfully becoming aware of something . . .[12]

Even from his prison cell, Dostoevsky had strained to glimpse the dawn.

Now, however, facing imminent death, Dostoevsky greedily gathered in final impressions of the world. Then he heard the drum roll that to the experienced military ear denoted a suspension of the execution. He listened as his death sentence was commuted to four years of hard labour and demotion to the rank of private in a Siberian army unit. Three days later, on Christmas Eve, clamped in heavy leg-irons, he was carted out of St Petersburg, passing on his way the house of his publisher Andrei Kraevsky, its windows aglow with celebrations of the feast.

Like Dostoevsky, we remain riveted to the moment of his suspenseful expectation of death, a moment captured in a remarkable letter Dostoevsky wrote to his brother Mikhail that very same day, 23 December 1849:

Brother! I have not been grieving and I have not lost spirit. Life everywhere is life, life is in ourselves and not in something external. Alongside of me will be people, and to be a *human being* among people and to remain so forever, not to grieve or falter whatever the misfortunes – this is what life is about, that is its purpose. I have understood this. This idea has entered into my flesh and blood. It's true: that mind which created, which lived the superior life of art, which has understood and reconciled itself to the sublime needs of the spirit, that mind has been severed from my shoulders. I retain the memory and images which I have created but not yet made incarnate. They will torture me, it is true! But I still have my heart and that very flesh and blood, which can love, and suffer, and desire, and remember, and that is life after all! *On voit le soleil!* [. . .] Life is a gift, life is happiness; every minute could be a century of happiness. *Si jeunesse savait!* Now, changing my life, I am reborn in a new form. Brother! I swear to you that I shall not lose hope and shall keep pure my heart and soul. I shall be born again for the best. That is all my hope, all my comfort.[13]

Not only is Dostoevsky intent on putting a brave face on his sentence, he reaffirms his belief in the power of his art to change the world. All that is left to him are 'memory and images'; he has created them in his mind, but they have still to be made 'incarnate' in material life. That remains his hope and his duty.

One of the many remarkable aspects of this letter is that, at a moment of such extreme personal crisis, Dostoevsky should quote in French from Victor Hugo's *Last Day of a Man Condemned to Death* (1829). Does this mean that, like his characters, Dostoevsky had lost any ability to experience life directly, without the mediation of books? In fact, perhaps under Hugo's influence, Dostoevsky had been fascinated for some time with the way that, by projecting a definite end-point in time, execution deepens experience to an infinite degree, to the point of epiphany. Most notably, the protagonist of *White Nights* speaks of his dreaming as 'pronouncing sentence over himself',[14] and, in a passage omitted by Dostoevsky in later editions, ruminates: 'They say that the approximation of punishment causes in the criminal a true repentance and sometimes engenders pangs of conscience in even the most hardened heart.'[15] While Dostoevsky experienced his punishment as a profound emotional shock, with the other, morbidly curious part of his doubled consciousness he almost seems to have sought it out.

Poet and critic Vyacheslav Ivanov held that 'all of [Dostoevsky's] further revelations [. . .] were only attempts to communicate to the world [. . .] what was once revealed to him in a catastrophic inner experience.'[16] The notion of narrating one's own death – what Jacques Derrida called autothanatography – calls attention to the contradictions inherent in testimony.[17] *Martyrdom* is an authority achieved only at the moment the witness loses his life. Bartholomew bears his witness only at the very end of time. Dostoevsky dares to bear witness in time, but always on the brink of catastrophe, of apocalypse. Moreover he dares to do so (mostly) in fiction, which would appear to contradict the very notion of complete sincerity. Dostoevsky's near-execution made it impossible for him ever to present the healing image he desired. Like Lazarus and like Zosima, his witness retained the odour of death. However, Dostoevsky's execution, held in abeyance for over 30 years, also became the guarantor of his abiding contemporaneity.

In the camp Dostoevsky wore the Jack-of-Diamonds outfit of the common convict: a jacket that was half-grey and half-black with a yellow diamond on the back, supplemented with a matching cap in the summer and a coat with earmuffs and gloves in the winter. A young guard who served at the camp in Omsk recalled that Dostoevsky and his fellow Petrashevets Sergei Durov (1815–1869) were distinguished from the mass by 'indelible traces of upbringing and education', but that physically Dostoevsky appeared to suffer:

> Dostoevsky looked like a strong, squat and thick-boned worker, with good stature and military discipline. But the consciousness of his hard, hopeless fate seemed to turn him to stone. He was awkward, immobile and silent. His pale, thin, earthen-coloured face, covered in dark-red spots, never brightened with a smile, and his mouth opened only for short, gasping answers for work or service. He wore his hat on his forehead, down to his eyebrows, and he bore a gloomy, focused, unpleasant gaze, bending his head forwards and lowering his eyes to the ground.[18]

Dostoevsky had said that memories of his fleeting success and the immaterial images of his unwritten works would sustain him. Certainly nothing else would.

It is impossible for us to know what Dostoevsky experienced in his four years of incarceration in the labour camp in Omsk and how exactly these experiences affected him. Apart from the fictionalized account in *Notes from the Dead House* we have only the sketchiest of testimonies. In letters he described the hardships of life among common criminals: 'This is a crude mob, irritated and angry. Hatred for noblemen exceeds all bounds, and therefore they treated us with hostility and with ill-tempered joy at our grief.'[19] The convicts 'smell like pigs' and do 'swinish things' (some of a sexual nature), excusing themselves by saying 'I'm a living person, after all.' Amid the squalor he learned the value of solitude, 'otherwise in this enforced communism you'll become a misanthrope'.[20] He was stricken with an illness that was eventually diagnosed as epilepsy, though it might have been related to the nervous disorder from which he had previously suffered. 'Add to all these pleasures the near impossibility of having a book, and of needing to read surreptitiously whatever you get ahold of, the eternal enmity and arguments around you, the cursing, screaming, noise, chatter, always under guard, never alone, and all four years without change.'[21] To his younger brother Andrei he confessed that 'those four years I regard as a time when I was buried alive and enclosed in a coffin'.[22] He bore the physical and spiritual wound for the rest of his life.

At the same time it was a school of sorts. For one thing, Dostoevsky got to know a multitude of 'national types and characters [. . .] Enough for entire volumes': 'Amidst the robbers at the camp I, in four years, at last was able to discern some people. Would you believe: deep, strong, beautiful characters, and how joyful it is to discover gold underneath a rough crust.'[23] Moreover he had had time to think: 'my eternal concentration in myself, where I escaped from bitter reality, has brought forth fruit. I now have many needs and hopes which I did not suspect before [. . .] I need books and money.'[24] He asked his brother to send the Qur'an, Kant and Hegel.

Upon release from the camp in January 1854 Dostoevsky was enlisted in the fort at Semipalatinsk, now a major city – Semei – in northern Kazakhstan. After a time in the barracks Dostoevsky was able to live independently; he soon won promotion to officer rank and became active in local society, such as it was. Dostoevsky met the young civil servant Aleksandr Vrangel, whom he later called 'my friend at a time when I had no friends, witness of my endless fortune and terrible sorrow'.[25] In a detailed memoir Vrangel described this frontier town:

All buildings were wooden, made of logs, rarely covered over by planks. There were five or six thousand residents together with the garrison and the Asiatics – merchants from Qoqand, Bukhara, Tashkent and Kazan. Semi-nomadic Kyrgyz lived on the left bank [of the Irtysh River], mostly in *yurts*, although some rich families had houses in which they wintered. There were about three thousand of them.

There was one Orthodox church in the town, the only stone building, and seven mosques. There was a large market yard, where caravans of camels and pack horses gathered, apart from the barracks, a government hospital and official buildings. There were no schools apart from one provincial schoolhouse. Even the dispensary was state-run. No stores apart from one haberdashery where you could find everything from a simple nail to Parisian perfume and a stock of cloth and material [. . .] Of course there was no bookshop: there were no readers.[26]

Though Dostoevsky had little good to say about Semipalatinsk, it clearly served as the basis for one of the few detailed landscapes in his fictional work, namely the epilogue to *Crime and Punishment*, where its emptiness describes the terrifying and redemptive promise of freedom.

After his years of prodigious writing and his fleeting fame, Dostoevsky no doubt struggled to accept his enforced silence; he was no willing ascetic. It is too easy to see the period as a catharsis that authorized Dostoevsky to adopt the role of spiritual guide. In fact the bowed man who emerged from imprisonment and exile was no less profane than the impudent youth who had disappeared from view years earlier. Still, Dostoevsky was changed by the camps in several respects. For the first time, at the age of 33, he seemed profoundly concerned with the prospect of family life. He met Maria Dmitrievna Isaeva as the wife of a local official with whom he became friendly. When the alcoholic Mr Isaev died in 1855, Dostoevsky courted the widow, who was still only 29. Having beaten off the attentions of a rival, Dostoevsky married her in 1857 and adopted her young son Pavel as his own. His ne'er-do-well stepson would remain a scourge to the end of Dostoevsky's life.

During this period Dostoevsky became increasingly monarchist in his political views. In 1870 Dostoevsky recalled that, with the outbreak of the Crimean War (1853–1856), 'together with my comrades, the unfortunates and the soldiers, I had felt myself as a Russian, desired success for Russian arms [. . .] – though I still remained then with a strong ferment of the rotten Russian liberalism preached by shitters like the dung beetle Belinsky etc.'[27] Dostoevsky wrote some patriotic odes, which he submitted to his superiors as proof of his loyalty and for possible publication; the last of the three known poems was written at the conclusion of the Crimean War and begins:

The awesome war falls silent!
An end to the cruel combat! . . .

Raising the daring, haughty gauntlet,
Insulted in its sacred emotions,
Rus' awoke, trembling with wrath,
To fight the desperate enemy
And it reaped with valourous sword
The fruit of the bloody harvest.
Enriching with its sacred blood
Its fields in righteous battle,
The Russian land welcomes
Peace with Europe, achieved in war.[28]

When news of these poems reached St Petersburg Dostoevsky became the object of derision. In fact, his personal devotion to the imperial family seems to have been sincere. Dostoevsky had had personal contact with Nicholas I not only during his military service in Petersburg but also during his arrest, confinement and clemency, all of which occurred under the personal supervision of the emperor. His patriotism strengthened with the accession to the throne of Alexander II in 1855, whom Dostoevsky called 'our angelic emperor'. In later years Dostoevsky twice wrote to Alexander II and became a mentor of sorts to the crown prince, the future Alexander III. His belief in the monarch was consistent with his need always to attach his faith to concrete faces.

This attraction to the face is evident also in the Christian faith with which Dostoevsky left the camps. Having had a traditional religious upbringing, Dostoevsky had never really renounced his faith. In prison in St Petersburg he had read religious books, including accounts of pilgrimages to the Holy Land. In the camps his only book had been a New Testament, given to him by Nadezhda Fonvizina, the widow of one of the exiled Decembrists who had devoted her life to charitable work among convicts.[29] Upon his release Dostoevsky wrote to Fonvizina about his 'symbol of faith', which he had probably been mulling over for four long years, perhaps longer:

> there is nothing more beautiful, more profound, more sympathetic, more reasonable, more courageous, and more perfect than Christ, and there not only is not, but I tell myself with a jealous love that there cannot be. More than that: if someone succeeded in proving to me that Christ was outside the truth, and if, *indeed*, the truth was outside Christ, I would sooner remain with Christ than with the truth.[30]

Though this passage has become a classic statement of modern religious faith and a cornerstone of theological aesthetics, its strongly volitional nature leaves it just a stroke away from hysteria. Indeed just a few lines earlier Dostoevsky had effectively undermined its reliability:

> I will tell you that I am a child of my age, a child of unfaith and doubt, still now and even (I know) to the closing of my coffin. What terrible suffering this thirst for faith has cost me and still now costs me; in my soul it becomes stronger, the more reasons there are against it.

Dostoevsky's faith is not an escape from the forces of harsh necessity, but a contrarian challenge against them. This is both its power and its limitation.

Family, patriotism, religion: all three elements of this essentially conservative mindset issue directly from the artist's attempt to compose a new image for a new time. However, they also dramatize the metaphysical stakes that Dostoevsky's artistic venture was playing for in his art. If the image were to be the source of redemption, its failure would not only leave Dostoevsky's protagonists hermetically sealed in their own consciousness: it would imply a nihilistic negation of finding meaning in the universe. For the time being Dostoevsky drew on his new values as sources of artistic power, while avoiding undermining them with the unpredictable logic that ruled his art.

In late 1855 Dostoevsky was promoted back to junior officer rank, which freed him from living in the barracks and allowed him to engage in some writing. Bursting with ideas that he had carried through his hardships, at first Dostoevsky struggled to give them form. He tried desperately to catch up with the times, though in near-total isolation from the cultural centres he was wholly reliant on the press. The first new work Dostoevsky completed was the story 'Uncle's Dream', based around an anecdote concerning a senile prince who enlivens a provincial town by his arrival. He is manipulated by a dictatorial society lady into proposing marriage to her daughter Zinaida, the local beauty, only for the prince to decide (not without help from the daughter's previous suitor) that it was all a dream, albeit a very pleasant one. Though he appears to have enjoyed the work, Dostoevsky admitted writing the story 'at post haste' and it received very little notice.[31]

The cynical ambitions of the locals in 'Uncle's Dream' show Dostoevsky to be setting the romantic idealism of his younger days against a more hard-nosed realism. Still, despite it all, Dostoevsky retains his optimism regarding the aesthetic image. The humourous social anecdote of 'Uncle's Dream' is interrupted by a subplot concerning Zinaida's former lover, the young teacher Vasily, who loses her by betraying her trust. On his deathbed Vasily confesses to his sustaining dream:

> of becoming some great poet and to print in *Otechestvennye*
> *zapiski* the greatest poem that has ever been in the world.
> I planned to pour out my feelings in it, all my soul, so that
> wherever you were I would still be with you, I would ceaselessly

remind you of myself through my verse, and my greatest dream would be for you to think of me and say, 'No! he was not as bad a person as I thought.'[32]

In this world it seems the only hope for soulful communication lies with the press, represented here by the journal of Dostoevsky's mendacious former editor Andrei Kraevsky.

The second work by which Dostoevsky announced his return was *The Village Stepanchikovo and its Inhabitants: From the Notes of an Unknown Author*, which appeared in Kraevsky's *Otechestvennye zapiski* in November and December 1859. Originally conceived as a comedic drama, the novel is narrated by a young scholar, Sergei, who travels to the estate of his uncle Egor Ilyich Rostanev, a retired colonel and widower. He finds his uncle's household a 'madhouse', 'bedlam', ruled over by the narrow-minded sponger Foma Fomich Opiskin, who has manipulated his way to a dictatorial hold over the other inhabitants. The novel consists of a rollicking string of hilarious incidents over two days, culminating in the uncle's revolt against Foma Fomich and his betrothal to the young governess. Comparable to Molière's *Tartuffe*, the novel is mostly a mugs' gallery punctuated by brilliant comic set-pieces.

The Village Stepanchikovo describes a world ruled over by a petty and malevolent deity. Much of the action takes place in the idyllic garden of the country estate, which the orphaned narrator remembers from childhood sojourns, but for the most part this is a grotesquely fallen paradise, the hidden corners of which are populated by dimwitted failures who concoct outrageous romantic schemes. However, a redemptive promise is still evident in the garden's design when the uncle recalls the radiant moments of Sergei's childhood:

'Wondrous, wondrous creator! . . You must remember this garden well, Sergei: how you played and gambolled here when you were little! I remember when you were little', he added, looking at me with an inexplicable expression of love and happiness. 'You were only forbidden to approach the pond alone. Do you remember once, in the evening, my deceased Katya called you and began to caress you . . . You had been running in the garden before this and were all flush; your hair was so fair, in curls . . . She played with them and said: "It is good that you took him in, the orphan". Do you remember or not?'

'A bit, uncle.'

'It was still evening, and the sun shone on you both so brightly, and I sat in the corner and smoked my pipe and watched you both . . .'[33]

As so often in Dostoevsky, redemption is a matter of illumination, refracted by the impressions held in one's memory.

Despite his consciousness of its shortcomings, Dostoevsky's hopes for the work were linked especially to its presentation of 'two vastly typical characters which I have created and notated over five years, which have been flawlessly sculpted (in my opinion), and which are fully Russian characters and have been poorly indicated thus far in Russian literature'.[34] The novel gives early versions of major characters in the later novels. The uncle is a prototype of Stepan Trofimovich, the weak-willed progenitor of the young nihilists in *Demons*. The lackey Vidoplyasov is an early version of Smerdyakov, the murderous fourth Karamazov brother. Foma Fomich is in many respects a first sketch of the Underground Man, though his manipulative self-humiliation is only vaguely linked to contemporary ideologies: he is reputed to have been a writer who 'suffered for the truth', but in fact he is a failed writer (his surname, Opiskin, means 'spelling mistake') with perverse ideas about literature.[35] The novel ends up less a satire of society than a parody of literature. The ridiculously named Vidoplyasov writes in a genre he calls 'yelps'. (The genre has been continued by 'Vidoplyasov's Yelps', one of Ukraine's pre-eminent pop groups.) Finally the narrator himself, though identified as a mineralogist, is also a young author, and it is his rather hesitant notes we read.

The novel reveals Dostoevsky to be still obsessed with Gogol, for whom he had both sincere adulation and an intense sense of rivalry. As Yuri Tynyanov demonstrated, some of Foma Fomich's most outrageous comments are paraphrased from Gogol's *Selected Passages from Correspondence with Friends*, the book Belinsky was responding to in the letter Dostoevsky was caught disseminating in 1849. It is very curious to find Dostoevsky returning to this polemic ten years later. It suggests that Dostoevsky was still puzzling how best to respond to the radical ideas that he had encountered in the late 1840s. Contemplating *The Village Stepanchikovo*'s lack of success with editors, Dostoevsky admitted that 'it lacks external effect'.[36] One of those editors, Dostoevsky's former champion Nikolai Nekrasov, claimed that Dostoevsky was 'finished' as a writer. In fact he was just beginning. Though of limited ambition, the two post-exile works provide hints of a new, radically metaphysical poetics with which Dostoevsky finally made an indelible impression on the reading public.

3

The Name

'Gloomy and cold, with stone houses, no movement, no interest, not even a library to speak of. A real prison!'[1] Thus did the ancient town of Tver appear to Dostoevsky upon his return to European Russia in August 1859. Still prohibited from living in either capital city, he had no plans to make a home elsewhere. 'Although I am sitting in Tver I am still *continuing to wander*', he wrote to his brother Mikhail on 19 September.[2]

Nonetheless, in close proximity to both Moscow and St Petersburg, with letters reaching their addressees in a day instead of two weeks, Dostoevsky finally found himself in the midst of metropolitan literary culture. Dostoevsky set about reclaiming and, perhaps, redeeming the promise that his name already signified to his contemporaries, despite his long silence, the minor scandal of his patriotic odes and the flat reception of his new fictions. First he planned to gather the writings that had originally made his name, improving them wherever necessary. This was especially true of *The Double*, whose flaws Dostoevsky now recognized, but in which he still placed great faith: 'this correction, complete with a preface, will be worth a *new novel!* They will finally see what *The Double* is!'[3] He placed great hope on his new novel *The Insulted and the Injured*, which promised to be 'full of effects and passion'. He also seemed intent on capitalizing on his experiences as a convict. Even as he left Siberia he began planning a new work, *Notes from the Dead House*, in an utterly original style; as he wrote to his brother on 9 October 1859:

My personality will disappear. They are the notes of an unknown man; but I guarantee they will be interesting. There will be the most capital interest. They will be serious, gloomy, humorous, and colloquial conversation in the prison style [. . .] and the representation of people about whom literature has never even heard; they will be touching and, finally, most importantly, they will bear my name.[4]

Having survived his imprisonment physically and having undergone a personal renewal, Dostoevsky now set about remaking himself as writer.

While in Semipalatinsk he had repeatedly declared his intention to allow his works to gestate and mature before printing them, but he quickly returned to his old habit of underestimating the time he needed for this to occur. Writing to his brother on 1 October 1859, Dostoevsky said he planned to review all of his old works, submit the corrected text to the censor's office and commence printing the first volume in January 1860; to revise *The Double* by mid-December and prepare it for the second volume in late February; and to follow both of these closely with *The Village of Stepanchikovo* in a third volume. Eight days later he announced that he would also finish *Notes from the Dead House* by 1 December and submit the first part of *The Insulted and the Injured* in March or April.[5] Though the two volumes of his *Collected Works* (without *The Double*) were in stores by the end of March 1860, these other projects would occupy Dostoevsky for the next two years. The inevitable delay was a blow not only to his ego, but also to his finances, since he was constantly borrowing money against his anticipated earnings. The stakes of his wager on his name continued to grow.

Eager to contribute to the ambitious reform of Russian society under Alexander II, in 1860 the Dostoevsky brothers launched a monthly intellectual review, *Vremya* (Time). The enterprise

Unknown photographer, *Fyodor Dostoevsky*, c. 1861.

depended in large part on the entrepreneurial skill Mikhail Dostoevsky had demonstrated in the tobacco business he had begun after resigning his commission in 1849. Mikhail hit on the idea of including a small gift in his boxes of cigarettes, which he sold as 'cigarettes with a surprise'. His journal also had a surprise: its intellectual leader was Fyodor Dostoevsky, who in late December was permitted to move back to Petersburg and whose name, Mikhail said, was 'worth a million'.

The announcement which Fyodor Dostoevsky wrote for *Vremya* positioned the journal as the site of a nascent ideology of national unity, which soon became known as 'native-soil-ism' (*pochvennichestvo*). Anticipating an end to serfdom, Dostoevsky hailed the entrance into public life of 'millions of Russians [who] will bring their fresh untapped forces and will say their new word'.[6] Lamenting the fissure between the educated class and the 'people' (*narod*) that had opened up under Peter I, Dostoevsky praised the simple folk for having sought original forms of life, though he admits they were sometimes 'disfigured' (*bezobrazny*).[7] Alexander II's reforms are taken as an acknowledgement that 'we are incapable of fitting ourselves into one of the Western forms of life, engendered and developed by Europe from its own national principles, foreign and opposed to ours, just as we could not wear someone else's clothes that have been sewn to another's measurements.' 'Our task', he concludes, 'is to create for ourselves a new form, our own, native to us, taken from our own soil, taken from the national spirit and from national principles', albeit a form that has been broadened and enriched by contact with Europe.[8]

The new challenges were summed up for Dostoevsky in the word 'positive' (*polozhitel'nyi*), the signal term of the 1860s. The new generation of radicals adopted the word to denote their devotion to empirical reality (as in philosophical positivism) – and their implacable opposition to anything that smacked of the supernatural. In the writings of both Nikolai Dobrolyubov (1836–1861) and

Nikolai Chernyshevsky (1828–1889), this often resulted in a crass utilitarianism summed up in the phrase 'a pair of boots is superior to Pushkin'. Dostoevsky adapted the term 'positive' to his own uses, stressing the need for palpable social change to be rooted in acts of imagination and impressed on individuals through artistic form.

The means for achieving this task Dostoevsky saw first and foremost in literature, a term that included fiction, journalism and other modes of discourse and allowed him to declare complete independence from established 'antipathies and biases'.[9] Dostoevsky's attempt to position himself above the ideological fray, to maintain a kind of literary nobility, is evident in his dealings with other writers whose talents he acknowledged. On 3 November 1862 Dostoevsky complained to Nikolai Nekrasov about the latter's refusal to contribute poems to *Vremya*:

1) how can you, such a famous man in literature, tremble before some inchoate and (in nature) fleeting and baseless opinion? 2) Why would participation in our journal compromise you and feed rumours that you have betrayed Chernyshevsky? Is our journal really retrograde?[10]

On 23 December 1863 Dostoevsky wrote in a similar vein to Ivan Turgenev (1818–1883), who was afraid of tarnishing his credit with the progressive youth (earned mostly with *Fathers and Sons*) by publishing a tale of the supernatural:

Why do you think, Ivan Sergeevich (if indeed you do think so), that your 'Ghosts' are not timely and will be misunderstood? On the contrary, the talentless drones that have been imitating the masters for six years have reduced the positive trend to such vulgarity that they themselves would be glad for a purely poetic work [. . .] I even know the example of one utilitarian (a nihilist) who, though he does not like your work, has said that he can't put it down and that it makes a strong impression [. . .] So, the whole business consists in the question: does the fantastic have the right to exist in art? [. . .] Such pictures as the cliff etc. are hints at an elemental and as yet unresolved idea (the same idea that exists throughout nature), which might not resolve people's problems, but which now causes people to long and fear, though they cannot tear themselves away. No, this idea is more than timely and such fantastic things are *extremely positive*.[11]

Writing confidentially to his brother three months later, Dostoevsky found the story full of 'something disgusting, sick, geriatric, *unbelieving* in its impotence, in a word, typical Turgenev with his convictions', but reasserted his view that 'poetry will redeem a lot'.[12]

Another way that Dostoevsky sought to rise above ideological clichés was by serving as an objective chronicler of cultural events. In February 1864 Dostoevsky implored Mikhail to include in their journal (now renamed *Epokha* [Epoch]) a section called 'Literary Chronicle' comprising 'a list of all books and translations that have appeared in the last month, but only *all* of them without exception [. . .] a full catalogue with necessary explanations about published books' and a bimonthly 'bibliographical overview of other journals [. . .] a list of all the articles that have appeared over two months in journals and newspapers'.[13] Even in his peak years as a novelist Dostoevsky retained this desire to measure the pulse of society, most notably through the *Writer's Diary* he initiated in 1873. Such day-to-day engagement with society signified a particular kind of freedom for Dostoevsky; even Dmitry Karamazov, facing deportation to Siberia, dreams of publishing a newspaper. At the same time, the newspaper would arm Dostoevsky with knowledge that would allow him to rise above 'tendency' in his fictions.

The Dostoevsky brothers were not ultimately successful in their rather utopian designs. *Vremya* was closed in 1863, leaving debts and broken promises. Its successor *Epokha* was beset from the beginning by debts and delays even before the sudden death of Mikhail in June 1864, which left Dostoevsky in such a desperate emotional and financial position that for years he became, in his words, a 'literary proletarian'.[14]

In May 1860 Dostoevsky thought he would finish it in three months, but amid all his activities it was only on 9 July 1861 that he placed a full stop at the end of *The Insulted and the Injured*. The delay meant that the novel was completed only after Alexander II announced the emancipation of the serfs on 5 March 1861, and after Turgenev published his most successful novel, *Fathers and Sons*, which posed a generational conflict between the 'men of the 1840s' (such as Belinsky and Nekrasov) and a new, more radical youth (typified by Nikolai Dobrolyubov and Nikolai Chernyshevsky). From the very beginning Dostoevsky admitted clear parallels between his new novel and *Poor Folk*, as if he had decided to respond to the changed social situation by rewriting his breakthrough novel. The experience showed Dostoevsky how much catching up he still had to do.

The Insulted and the Injured centres on the Ikhmenevs, a family of old noble stock who have been impoverished, in part because of the gambling of paterfamilias Nikolai Sergeevich Ikhmenev. They adopt the orphan Ivan Petrovich (we never learn his surname), who becomes a writer and, like Dostoevsky, enjoys early success with a novel that sounds just like *Poor Folk*. Ivan and the Ikhmenevs' daughter Natasha grow up as siblings and friends and are, in time, betrothed to be married. Upon reaching maturity, however, Natasha abandons Ivan for Aleksei Valkovsky, the weak-willed but charming scion of the Ikhmenevs' neighbour and rival Prince Pyotr Valkovsky. Saddled with debt, the manipulative elder Valkovsky sets up a more advantageous match for his son and eventually compels him to abandon Natasha, her reputation in shreds.

As in *The Village Stepanchikovo* Dostoevsky saw the value of his new novel in the introduction into literature of new social types, mainly those suffering from changes to the meaning of their hereditary nobility. For the elder Valkovsky hereditary nobility is a commodity that signifies (and, to a degree, enables) the accumulation of wealth. Nikolai Sergeevich, by contrast, sees his daughter's potential marriage to Valkovsky junior as 'the main shame' and appeals to her 'noble pride' as the strongest possible 'response to society'.[15] While this dilemma would remain important to Dostoevsky and his fictional world, its presentation here seems somewhat archaic. Dostoevsky later admitted that his rush to finish the novel had left the characters 'dolls, not people [. . .] walking books, not faces'.[16]

As in Dostoevsky's pre-exilic fictions, the characters put much stock in the healing image, like the locket with a portrait of Natasha at eight years of age that her parents treasure and adore:

> Nikolai Sergeevich and I commissioned it from an itinerant artist, He was a good artist and he depicted her as a cupid: she had fair, fluffed hair then; he represented her in a light muslin blouse so that her body shone through, and she came out so pretty that one can't tear one's eyes away. I asked the artist to give her little wings, but he didn't agree.[17]

Like this portrait, embedded in forms that were fast growing obsolete, Dostoevsky's fictional world seems to lag behind the pressures that were rapidly reforming people's lives in Russia, and this lag tempers the impression the novel makes. As his friend Filipp Masloboev says about Ivan's novel: 'as soon as I read it, brother, I almost became a reputable man! Almost; but then I mulled it over and preferred to remain in disrepute.'[18] More effective is the image and story of Nelly, an adolescent girl whom Ivan saves from prostitution. Ivan will always remember the 'dear image of the poor girl [. . .] as an image, as a picture'.[19] The story she tells just before her death, which reveals her to be the secret daughter of Prince Valkovsky and his English lover, reconciles the Prince's various victims. It proved to be a popular set piece; one reviewer copied it out in full and Dostoevsky used it for a public reading as late as 14 December 1879, just a year before his death.

Rooted in his youthful sentimentalism, at the same time *The Insulted and the Injured* shows Dostoevsky lurching towards the poetics of his later novels, albeit in a somewhat haphazard manner. First there are the protagonists' uncontrollable emotions, most notably Natasha's attraction to Aleksei:

> I am glad to be his slave, his voluntary slave; to put up with everything, everything he subjects me to as long as he remains with me, as long as I can look at him! [. . .] I fear no torments from him! I will know that I suffer *because of him* . . .[20]

Though self-destructive, this love is respected as an unconditional self-abnegation that paradoxically provides power over one's beloved; as Ivan Petrovich comments, 'She anticipated the pleasure of loving to the point of self-oblivion and tormenting one's beloved in pain precisely because one loves.'[21] Ivan adopts an equally masochistic role, offering to ferry letters between his fiancée and her lover.[22] Dostoevsky identifies some of the central paradoxes of his fictional world, for instance the way in which virtue engenders its own brand of egoism, or the way that corporal sickness frequently accompanies – and perhaps facilitates – spiritual health. For the moment, however, this charting of the emotional perversity of modernity awaits its philosophical explanation as a form of nihilism, which first appears in *Notes from Underground* and is most fully established in *Demons*. Dostoevsky seems not to take seriously the emerging radical ideologies which Natasha's cousins Lyova and Borya pick up at the circle of the ridiculously named Bezmygin, which sound a lot like the 'rational egoism' espoused in Dostoevsky's day by Dobrolyubov and Chernyshevsky: 'If you want to be respected, first of all respect yourself.'[23]

A similar irony tinges the sense of 'mystical terror' which the narrator defines as

> the gravest, most tortuous fear of something that I cannot define, something unknowable and absent from the order of things, but which seems likely to occur immediately, which will come to me as if in spite of all the arguments of reason and will stand before me as an irrefutable fact, terrible, disfigured and implacable.[24]

This sense is most closely associated with the subplot concerning Nelly and her grandfather Smith, who dies in Ivan's arms. Ivan is puzzled by his own attachment to Nelly, which he struggles to explain by reference to 'the mysteriousness of the entire situation, the impression made on me by Smith, or the fantastic nature of my own mood'.[25] In fact, the characters' mysticism is also made light of, for instance when the young prince Valkovsky attends a spiritualist seance where Julius Caesar signs his name as 'something like "drip"'.[26] Though Ivan Petrovich's attunement to the fantastic opens his eyes to new, redemptive potentials in the world, he has trouble forming this intuition into effective images strong enough to survive scepticism and ridicule. He is, in Dostoevsky's terms, a poet, but not an artist.

This is quite a problem for Dostoevsky, considering that Ivan Petrovich is not only the protagonist of the novel, but is also its narrator, who consciously shapes his experiences into

> one of those depressing and tortuous stories that so frequently and imperceptibly, almost mysteriously occur under the heavy

Petersburg sky, in the dark, hidden corners of an enormous city, amid the heady tide of life, the crude egoism, the conflicting interests, the glum perversion, the secret crimes, among all this pure hell of pointless and abnormal life . . .[27]

Like Dostoevsky's other first-person narratives, from *The Double* and 'White Nights' to *Notes from Underground* and *The Adolescent*, the novel is constrained by the limits of its protagonist's understanding and by the impenetrability of modern urban life. Since Ivan Petrovich shares so many characteristics with his creator it is tempting to see the novel as Dostoevsky's reflection on the limits of his own narrative method, such as the extremity of emotional states and the frequency of sudden turns of plot, limits that were reinforced by the pressures of serial publication. When preparing the novel for a new edition in 1865 he pruned it of some of the more conspicuous signs of melodramatic excess, such as the heroine's frequent fainting fits. *The Insulted and the Injured* registered these pressures and made clear to Dostoevsky the need for the emergent new world of his imagination to find commensurate new forms of narrative.

The most effective account of the world is provided by Masloboev, one of Dostoevsky's great comic creations, a fixer, sometime private eye and inveterate drunkard. He attributes his perceptive judgements to his studies in 'physiognomistics', while his success in gathering information he explains by his readiness to accept bribes: '*Je prend mon bien, oú je le trouve* [I take my goods where I find them], and only in this sense am I similar to Molière', he says. But above all he claims to have a richer imagination than the writer Ivan Petrovich: 'I can get drunk, lie down on my sofa (and I have a fine sofa, with springs) and think that I am, for instance, some kind of Homer or Dante, or a Friedrich Barbarossa [. . .] I have imagination while you have reality.'[28] Masloboev operates in the shadows of the world, placing his trust not in the radiant images of orphans but in more tangible currencies. Concealing as much as he reveals, masking his commitments with irrepressible irony, Masloboev provides a prototype for Dostoevsky's future narrators.

Like *White Nights*, *The Insulted and the Injured* projects a healing image only to unmask it as a fragile spectre incapable of asserting itself in the real world. In the character of Nelly, who complains to Ivan that his novel is 'untrue', Dostoevsky suggests that the healing image can itself be suspicious of its ability to serve the causes of truth and justice.[29] Caught between his impulses towards fiction and journalism, between making an impression and capturing the truth, Dostoevsky faced an entire host of aesthetic problems. It was to resolve these problems that, in the middle of 1861, Dostoevsky headed back to the Dead House.

It was in his fictionalized memoir of prison life that Dostoevsky began in earnest to experiment with new modes of storytelling. Dostoevsky had conceived this work early in his Siberian sojourn, when he had kept a notebook of phrases and words, some of which made it into *The Village Stepanchikovo*. As early as 18 January 1856 Dostoevsky wrote to his old friend Apollon Maikov that 'In hours when I have nothing to do I note things from my memories of being in the prison camp, the more curious things. Actually there's not that much of a purely personal nature here.'[30] He began printing sections of *Notes from the Dead House* in September 1860, before *The Insulted and the Injured* was in full gear, but he set it aside to write the novel and returned to it only in July 1861. By this time it was already beginning to overshadow everything else Dostoevsky had written – and everything he would write for some time.

Notes from the Dead House is justly regarded as the first great work in the Russian literature of captivity after Archpriest Avvakum's autobiography from the 1670s. Like Avvakum in his *Life*, and like

Dostoevsky, *Portrait of an Unknown Man*, 1863.

Aleksandr Solzhenitsyn in his 'experiment in literary investigation' *The Gulag Archipelago* (1973), Dostoevsky found himself obliged to invent a new literary form for a world that refused to submit to conventional means of literary representation. Instead of an authoritative narrator, Dostoevsky entrusted the work to the eccentric Aleksandr Petrovich Goryanchikov, a former inmate whose 'notes' have allegedly been recovered and published by an unnamed editor who selects from the 'disconnected' description of camp life 'another tale, some strange and frightful memories, drafted unevenly, fitfully, as if under some kind of coercion'.[31]

The narrative begins with an overwhelming sense of spatial and temporal disorientation, claustrophobia and oblivion, amid which inmates struggle to restore some kind of order. One common strategy is to force some kind of resolution by attempting escape or provoking the guards into a response; the result is a perpetual rhythm of crime and retribution that traps everyone in an adversarial logic as both potential victim and executioner; recalling the Marquis de Sade, Goryanchikov posits this logic as typical of 'modern man'.[32] In search of an alternative frame of reference, one inmate takes to counting the logs in the prison wall: 'Each log represented a day; every day he counted out a single log and thus, by the remaining number of uncounted logs, could clearly see how many days remained for him in the prison until his work term was up. He was sincerely glad whenever he completed a side of the hexagon.'[33] Goryanchikov also ends up recovering some kind of structure in the cyclical calendar of camp life, which roughly follows the natural sequence of seasons and the Christian story of birth, death and resurrection. Goryanchikov's narrative is the same kind of attempt to reclaim measures of judgement and criteria of discernment in a situation of total negation, of nihilism. Like Dostoevsky's subsequent experiments in the genre of 'notes' – from the underground, of impressions of a summer trip to Western Europe, right up to the novel *The Adolescent* – this is a story in which narrative is no longer possible, a pure duration of language, what Roland Barthes called 'writing degree zero'.[34]

In addition to the calendar and language, Goryanchikov is also able to find a measure of order in the faces of the men who surround him: 'Meeting them during [my] walks, I loved to peer into their sullen, branded faces and guess what they were thinking about.'[35] The work consists largely of a series of portraits of these individuals, from the hell-hole of the camp bathhouse to the yuletide pantomime, when 'a strange reflection of child-like joy and sweet, pure pleasure glowed on these furrowed, branded brows and cheeks, in the gazes of these hitherto so gloomy and sullen men, in these eyes which sparkled sometimes with terrible flame'.[36] But the moral change is fleeting, lasting only 'for a mere several minutes', and they are back in the barracks:

> I look at their pale faces, at their poor beds, at all of this impass-able nakedness and poverty, – I peer in, – and it is as if I want to make sure that it is not the continuation of a disfigured dream, but actual truth. But it is truth: I hear someone's groan; someone throws out his hand heavily and clangs his chains.[37]

The momentary illumination of faces which had previously redeemed the entirety of reality is no longer sufficient. In the camps Dostoevsky came to realize that it was not the face that gives the best measure of the man, but the entirety of his body. One can point to the story of Mikhailov – a 'well-imaged' consumptive with 'beautiful eyes' who passes away in Goryanchikov's presence in the hospital:

> He died around three o'clock in the afternoon, on a cold and clear day. I recall, the strong slanted rays of the sun simply penetrated the green, slightly frosted glass in the windows of our ward. An entire stream of them poured onto the unfortunate man.[38]

However the portrait of Mikhailov is also a frightening tale of the abandonment of the body by the spirit, a recurring motif in Dostoevsky's later fiction. The man's last act is to pull off the amulet around his neck, 'as if it also was a burden to him, worrying and pressing down on him'.[39] It was no longer enough for Dostoevsky to find a redemptive beauty in the faces of select individuals; he now needed to forge a form for the entirety of the human body and of human society. Instead of simply recouping his original career path, Dostoevsky would strike out in a wholly new direction.

4

The Wager

By 1862 Dostoevsky was well on his way to reclaiming the all-too brief fame he had enjoyed prior to his arrest in April 1849, but in addition to his purely literary ambitions he was now also conscious of a higher purpose, acquired during his time in the camps. Dostoevsky's works of the early 1860s represent his first attempts not only to escape the restrictive logic of the modern media, but also to create a Christian literature. As Dostoevsky's works make abundantly clear, this did not necessarily mean a literature about Christ, about the Christian church or even about Christian characters. Instead, Christianity infuses his work as a gesture, changing the quality of his images by setting them against an infinite horizon. The crucial decision was to cease projecting ideas onto fictional forms and to allow both form and idea to emerge viscerally from his raw experience. Ceding a degree of control over his own imagination, Dostoevsky entered into a kind of wager on form, trusting that it would allow him to overcome the disfigurement of his times and milieux.

Dostoevsky's most extended piece of political writing in the 1860s was *Winter Notes on Summer Impressions*, which was serialized in *Vremya* in early 1863. It is based on Dostoevsky's journey through Germany, France, England and Italy from 7 June to 23 August 1862, his first ever journey abroad, for which he required special permission from the police, who had him under observation as a former convict. *Winter Notes on Summer Impressions* was his most sustained piece of social commentary from the 1860s, which amounted to a thorough and impassioned attack on the foundations of modern society as exemplified by Britain, France and Germany. Dostoevsky was roundly horrified with what he found in contemporary Europe, with its twin facets of bourgeois comfort and urban squalor, a duality that struck Dostoevsky most in London:

> This city, bustling day and night and as endless as the sea, the squeal and roar of machines, these railways set above buildings (and soon beneath buildings), this boldness of entrepreneurship, this apparent disorder, which in essence is the height of bourgeois order, this poisoned Thames, this air saturated with coal, these magnificent squares and parks, the horrific corners of the city like Whitechapel, with its semi-naked, savage and hungry population. The City with its millions and worldwide trade, the Crystal Palace, the Great Exhibition . . . Yes, the Exhibition is remarkable. You feel the horrific power that has connected here all these countless people from all over the world into a single herd; you feel that here something has already been achieved, that this is victory and celebration. It's even as if you begin to be afraid of something.[1]

It is not the city itself, horrible as it is, but the smug self-satisfaction with the 'achieved ideal' that Dostoevsky finds most frightening. Set against the child prostitutes of Haymarket, Western bourgeois capitalism is an echo of Babylon and a portent of the Antichrist. It is a vision that would remain with Dostoevsky for the rest of his life.

Meanwhile in St Petersburg, writing from the prison cell he had occupied since July 1862, Nikolai Chernyshevsky was publishing his subversive novel *What Is to Be Done?* in the rival journal *Sovremennik* (The Contemporary). This was a major oversight on the part of the censors, because *What Is to Be Done?* was a transparent programme for the radical reformation of Russian society under the leadership of heroic individuals of iron will. The views that brought Chernyshevsky to this vision were close to utilitarianism, meaning that actions should be judged in terms of their expediency. Naturally, utilitarians must assume that we can know the standard against which expediency can be measured; usually it was economic well-being. In Chernyshevsky's rational egotism, utilitarianism as a social theory coincided with altruism as a maxim for individual action and socialism as a social goal; in essence, it is in everyone's individual self-interest that the whole of society flourish. Chernyshevsky's novel implied revolutionary action as a means of establishing this self-evident truth.

Appearing at the same time, Dostoevsky's *Winter Notes* share major concerns with Chernyshevsky's novel, albeit viewed from the opposite end of the political spectrum. Both works feature the image of the Crystal Palace, the vast iron-and-glass structure created in London for the 1851 Great Exhibition and left standing for 25 years afterwards as a museum of – and monument to – the aspirations and power of modernity. In Chernyshevsky's novel the Crystal Palace appears in the heroine Vera Pavlovna's 'fourth dream' as the home for inhabitants of a future paradise of joyful labour and abundant, equal rewards; both the natural landscape and the social structure have been transformed after everyone suddenly realizes that they should strive for 'what is useful': 'It is only necessary to be cautious, to be able to organize well and to learn how to use resources to the greatest advantage', explains Vera Pavlovna's guide.[2] For Dostoevsky, Chernyshevsky's novel was not merely a mistaken ideology; it signalled a moral failure to hold society to its own highest potential – and was therefore a fatal compromise with conscience.

Dostoevsky's rather extravagant rhetoric should not deflect attention from his mercilessly incisive critique of modern Western society, which stands in importance and power alongside those of Karl Marx (1818–1883) and Friedrich Nietzsche (1844–1900). No less than Marx, a near contemporary, Dostoevsky recognized, from *The Double* on, how the force of capital was becoming translated into new arrays of power, desire and violence. Nowhere more than in Dostoevsky's fiction does one see a more rigorous analysis of Marx's proposition that, in bourgeois modernity, 'all that is solid melts into air'.[3] After witnessing European society first-hand in 1862, Dostoevsky gained direct insight into the inevitable direction of Russian society in its latest push for modernization. Beginning with *Crime and Punishment* (almost exactly contemporary with Marx's *Capital*, which appeared in 1867), Dostoevsky set his economic and social critique within a consideration of the possible responses: the criminal (Raskolnikov), the passionate (*The Idiot*), the revolutionary (*Demons*) and the religious (*The Brothers Karamazov*). As different as their analyses and solutions were, both Dostoevsky and Marx sought to identify the iron forces of necessity in order to establish the conditions of a new freedom.

In addition to his novels *Notes from the Dead House* and *The Insulted and the Injured* and the political commentary of *Winter Notes on Summer Impressions*, Dostoevsky also printed in his journal *Vremya* a series of unsigned theoretical essays on literature which rigorously formulate the influential aesthetic theory that, explicitly or implicitly, Dostoevsky held to throughout his life. Wide-ranging and polemical, these essays are addressed against the dominant utilitarian view of the two Nikolais, Chernyshevsky and Dobrolyubov, proposing aesthetics and culture as an autonomous realm of human endeavour capable of reconciling contradictions and disputes in other realms: 'Our new Rus' has realized that the only cement, the only connection, the only soil on which everything will gather and be reconciled is universal spiritual reconciliation, the beginning of which lies in education [*obrazovanie*].'[4]

At the heart of the word 'education', which can also mean 'culture', is the term 'image' (*obraz*). Robert Louis Jackson was the first to identify Dostoevsky's systematic use of the terms *image* (*obraz*) and *disfiguration* (*bezobrazie*) as a central fulcrum of his entire aesthetic project.[5] But how would Dostoevsky's image differ from a purely imaginary and therefore innocuous construct like the utopia of Vera Pavlovna's fourth dream in Chernyshevsky's *What Is to Be Done*? Such flighty images eviscerate the reality they describe. Seeking a synthetic position between the aesthetes and the utilitarians, a position that would allow him to assert the image as ideal while acknowledging the material as its real condition and end, Dostoevsky clearly favoured the partisans of art for art's sake, whose view he formulated as follows:

> For example, such-and-such a man once, in his adolescence, when 'all the impressions of life were fresh', glanced at the Belvedere Apollo and the god was indelibly imprinted in his soul in his most majestic and endlessly beautiful image [. . .] There are many impressions in this world, of course, but it is not for nothing that this impression was special, the impression of a god. Not for nothing do these impressions remain for an entire life.[6]

These impressions are the secret to the positive impact of art:

> Therefore, if you assign a purpose to art ahead of time and determine how exactly it should be useful, then you might make a frightful mistake, so that instead of utility one might bring only harm, and therefore act against one's own interests, since the utilitarians demand utility, not harm. And since art most of all requires complete freedom, and freedom does not exist without calmness (any alarm is already unfreedom), then it follows that art should act quietly, clearly, without hurry, without distraction, having itself as a purpose and believing that any effect will turn to humanity's utility with time.[7]

Of course, Dostoevsky's own texts are eminently noisy, obscure, hurried and distracted. The Belvedere Apollo certainly never set foot near them.

Dostoevsky hardly fits the stereotype of 'art for art's sake', but there are striking parallels between his aesthetic statements and those of Walter Pater, who in an essay from 1868 described the power of art in terms Dostoevsky would have found familiar:

> we are all *condamnés*, as Victor Hugo says: we are all under sentence of death but with a sort of indefinite reprieve [. . .] we have an interval, and then our place knows us no more. Some spend this interval in listlessness, some in high passions, the wisest, at least among 'the children of this world', in art and song. For our one chance lies in expanding that interval, in getting as many pulsations as possible into the given time. Great passions may give us this quickened sense of life, ecstasy and sorrow of love, the various forms of enthusiastic activity, disinterested or otherwise, which come naturally to many of us. Only be sure it is passion – that it does yield you this fruit of a quickened, multiple consciousness. Of such wisdom, the poetic passion, the desire of beauty, the love of art for art's sake, has most. For art comes to you proposing frankly to give nothing but the highest quality to your moments as they pass, and simply for those moments' sake.[8]

Aside from the reference to Hugo's *Last Day of a Man Condemned to Death*, Pater's epicureanism might seem a world away from Dostoevsky, but there is evidence that the latter explicitly identified his aesthetic theory with the notion of 'art for art's sake'.[9] The point is, however, that Dostoevsky saw his suspended narratives as exceeding any theory, focusing attention on the interval in order to render accessible an infinite potentiality of time. In his earnest efforts to achieve positive social change, Dostoevsky was making a radical wager on form.

Written 'deep in the shadow of the dead house', in crucial respects *Notes from Underground* represents the culmination of the ideological duel between Dostoevsky and Chernyshevsky.[10] For one thing, it features the image of the Crystal Palace, which the Underground Man assails as a prisonhouse of the human will. In the Underground Man's thorough critique of Chernyshevsky's utilitarianism one senses Dostoevsky's own outrage at the replacement of morality by a form of economic calculation, which for him was an offensively reductive concept of reason. Most of all, though, the Underground Man appeals against the enthronement of economic well-being as the measure of expediency, saying that the idea of profit ignores the 'maximally profitable profit' – free will. Noting that the second part of *Notes from Underground*, 'Apropos of the Wet Snow', is set in the mid-1840s, around the time of Dostoevsky's literary debut with the sentimental epistolary novel *Poor Folk*, Joseph Frank has suggested that 'the novella is above all a diptych depicting two episodes of a symbolic history of the Russian intelligentsia'.[11] Breaking with the radicals of the 1860s, Dostoevsky was also confirming his break with his own past.

No less important was Dostoevsky's rejection of Chernyshevsky's utilitarian aesthetics. In the introduction to *What Is to Be Done?* Chernyshevsky confessed: 'I lack even a shade of artistic talent. I don't even have a good grasp of the language. But that's not important: read on, o kind public! Your reading of this book will not be devoid of utility. Truth is a good thing; it compensates for the failings of the writer who serves it.'[12] Dostoevsky could not separate truth from form in this manner, and never could he view a narrative as a vessel of ideas, obliquely stated. On the contrary, the ideological debates of the 1860s formed no more than material in which Dostoevsky was minting an image of much greater currency. Chernyshevsky characterized his task as the formation of a new public: 'If you were the public', Chernyshevsky explains to his knowing readers, 'I would no longer need to write. If you didn't exist, I couldn't write. But though you are not yet the public, you already exist among the public, so I must still and can already write.'[13] Chernyshevsky addresses his work to a new collective (one that eventually would take power in Russia and canonize him as their prophet). Dostoevsky, by contrast, uses the public sphere to speak directly to individuals in a work that is its own provocation and justification. Relinquishing the comfort of conventional form and medium, Dostoevsky wagered on the power of literature to enable moral and spiritual agency.

Notes from Underground was written over several months from the end of 1863 to early 1864. This was a tumultuous time in Dostoevsky's life. For one thing his wife Maria Dmitrievna lay dying of tuberculosis. Moreover, *Vremya* had suddenly been banned in May 1863 because of an article by Nikolai Strakhov (1828–1896) concerning the Polish uprising of that year. Dostoevsky always considered the closure of the journal a misunderstanding, writing to Turgenev on 17 June that the idea behind Strakhov's article was

> that the Poles so despise us as Barbarians, are so condescending to us with their European civilization, that no moral (i.e., solid) reconciliation is possible for us for a long time to come. But since the argument of the article was misunderstood they interpreted thus: that we *ourselves, for our own part* assert that the Poles are so superior to us with their civilization, while we are beneath them, so, naturally, they are right and we are guilty.[14]

The closure of the journal left the brothers Dostoevsky in debt to their creditors and subscribers, and they were frantically trying to get out its successor, *Epokha*. Dostoevsky felt that *Notes from Underground* (originally consisting of three parts) should be published all at once, but he struggled to get even the first part ('The Underground') into the inaugural issue of *Epokha* (January–February 1864), thereby delaying the launch of the journal until late March. In the third issue (technically for March, but released only in early May) an editorial note signed by Mikhail Dostoevsky informed readers that the 'continuation of F. M. Dostoevsky's tale *Notes from Underground* has been postponed to the next issue because of the author's illness'.[15] Part two, originally entitled 'A Tale Apropos of the Wet Snow', was published only in the fourth issue of the journal, which emerged belatedly in June 1864.

The delay was exacerbated by the censor's intervention in the first part of the *Notes* (especially, it would seem, what is now its tenth section). After perusing the journal Dostoevsky wrote furiously to his brother:

> the misprints are terrible and it would have been better not to print the penultimate chapter at all (the main one, where the very idea is enunciated) than to print it as it is, with forced phrases and contradicting itself. What can you do! The censors are pigs; wherever I ridiculed everything and at times blasphemed *for show* – that was let by, but where I derived from this the need for faith and Christ – this was prohibited. Are they, the censors, in a plot against the government or something?[16]

Since the manuscript has not survived we can only guess what exactly the censor excised and how accurately Dostoevsky characterized its significance; he was sometimes partial to exaggeration. We do know, however, that he began the second part, 'Apropos of the Wet Snow', with the knowledge that the positive elements of the Underground Man's rant had been lost, and one can thus surmise that this narrative was written to compensate for the excisions and provide the lacking 'need for faith and Christ'. Dostoevsky's inability to spell things out explicitly forced him to wager on the reader's ability to construct a finished image out of disparate elements. To a large degree any critical reading of

Notes from Underground rests on how one reconciles the two parts of the work: the diatribe and the narrative, the present and the past, the Underground Man and Liza.

The story of the work shows that it would be wrong to view it merely as a defence of free will and a rejoinder to Chernyshevsky, as it often was in the twentieth century by existentialists and Cold Warriors alike, who sometimes published the first part of *Notes from Underground* shorn of the longer, more complex second part. The editor's note accompanying the first publication contained an additional sentence that urged readers to regard the 'first fragment' as 'an introduction to the entire book, almost a preface'.[17] In letters to his brother Dostoevsky expressly argued against publishing the parts of the work separately from each other, fearing that this would upset the intricate linkages between them, which he likened to 'transitions' in music: 'The first chapter appears to be chatter, but suddenly in the last two chapters this chatter is resolved in an unexpected catastrophe', he wrote to Mikhail on 13 April 1864.[18] Further light is shed on the nature of this catastrophic resolution by another of Dostoevsky's intriguing comments to his brother concerning his work on the 'tale': 'In tone it is too strange, and the tone is shrill and wild; some people might not like it. Therefore it is necessary that poetry soften and redeem everything.'[19] We are left, then, with the question of where to seek the 'poetry' of part two and how it redeems the tale by proving 'the need for faith and Christ'.

After publishing *Winter Notes on Summer Impressions* in February and March 1863, and before beginning *Notes from Underground*, Fyodor Dostoevsky set off on a second trip to Western Europe at the beginning of August, where he planned to meet up with his lover, the 23-year-old Apollinaria Suslova. Though he claimed the trip was intended to treat his epilepsy, which had first afflicted him in prison in 1850, Dostoevsky also spent a lot of time in casinos, especially after he won a significant sum in mid-August which emboldened him to think that he had happened upon a reliable method, though it never again worked for him. Reaching Paris at the end of August, Dostoevsky was told by Apollinaria 'You have arrived a bit late': she had fallen in love with a young Spaniard.[20] However, Dostoevsky persuaded her to travel with him to Baden-Baden and then on to Italy, stopping in Turin, Genoa, Rome and Naples. On the ferry from Naples to Livorno on 13 October, Dostoevsky ran into Alexander Herzen (1812–1870), an émigré socialist who published the journal *Kolokol* (The Bell) in London. Introducing Apollinaria as his relative, Dostoevsky enjoyed a wide-ranging conversation with Herzen about Russia, Orthodox Christianity and the Slavophile movement. On his way back to Russia Dostoevsky stopped for a week in Bad Homburg, where he frittered away his remaining money and was forced to turn to Apollinaria and other friends to buy his railway ticket home. Left behind in Petersburg were Dostoevsky's terminally ill wife Maria and his wayward stepson Pavel Isaev, both of whom could have done with Dostoevsky's support, as could his brother Mikhail, who was reeling from the closure of *Vremya* by the government at the end of May. Dostoevsky kept an eye on all this as best as he could, but he was not present and was almost totally preoccupied.

Reprehensible as they were, Dostoevsky's actions in 1863 represent a continual assertion of freedom against the combined forces of necessity, whether financial, social or moral. Whether or not his epilepsy heightened his sensitivity to financial and erotic risk-taking, he always seemed ready and even eager to lodge a wager on the freedom of the future against the constraints of the present – not that this faith in providence was ever borne out materially. As Joseph Frank has written, by gambling Dostoevsky 'was para-doxically affirming his acceptance of the proper order of the universe as he conceived of it, and learning the same lesson as the under-ground man and all of his great negative heroes beginning with Raskolnikov who deludedly believe they can master and suppress the irrational promptings of Christian conscience'.[21] Dostoevsky's experiences in the summer of 1863 gave him the idea for a story which eventually became the novella *The Gambler* (1866), but before that they shaped the personality of the Underground Man, whose loss of faith in higher realities leads him constantly to hedge petty wagers with ever-diminishing returns. The problem was not to suppress the passion for risk by limiting desire even more stringently to the bounds of scientific or dogmatic reason, but rather to redeem desire by raising the stakes to the absolute, beyond what is commonly held to be rational or even possible.

How can the Underground Man's hedges yield these absolute winnings? The diatribe in the first part of the novella has tended to overpower the hesitant resolution provided in the sequel. In one of the very few contemporary responses, the radical writer Mikhail Saltykov-Shchedrin provided a parody of the *Notes*:

> the stage is neither dark nor light, but of some greyish hue; living voices are not audible, only a hissing, and living images are not visible, but it is as if bats are crossing through the twilight air. It is not a fantastic world but not a living one either, rather it is as if made of jelly.[22]

Responding to rumours about Dostoevsky's 'scandalous story', even Apollinaria Suslova expressed concern that Dostoevsky was becoming 'cynical'.[23] It must have pained him to hear this – one of the very few responses to the work that reached him – since he had put so much effort into the narrative refutation of the Underground Man's rant.

But then the refutation of the Underground Man by the prostitute Liza is not an argument at all. She is not empowered to speak for herself in the work. Like some of Dostoevsky's later heroines, most notably the titular character of 'The Gentle Creature' (from the *Writer's Diary* for 1876), Liza remains a mute image hung over the narrative, testifying to the possibility of redemption beyond speech. The crucial move here is that, though the Underground Man might presently be in a prison of his own construction, the investigation of his past reveals moments of lost potentiality, most notably when Liza extends her love. The work moves from the cold, hard facts of social conditions to an affirmation of spiritual causation. Liza's love is a silent pledge that he might still be able to redeem, though this would require a wager that he finds impossible: a wager on the Other.

Like so many of the experiences he related in his fiction, this was something Dostoevsky knew from experience. As he finished *Notes from Underground* Dostoevsky was close to despair. His beloved brother Mikhail died on 10 July 1864, endangering the journal *Epokha* and leaving Dostoevsky saddled with debts for the rest of his life. Even earlier, on 16 April 1864, Dostoevsky witnessed the death of his wife Maria. He wrote to Aleksandr Vrangel that she 'had loved me boundlessly, and I loved her also without measure, but we did not live happily together'.[24] Her death led Dostoevsky to record some of his loftiest words about human potential:

> Maria is lying on the table. Will I ever see Maria?
>
> To love another man *as oneself*, according to Christ's testament, is impossible. The law of the personality binds us on earth. The *I* gets in the way. Only Christ could, but Christ was the ideal eternal from the ages, to which man strives and should strive, according to the law of nature. At the same time after the appearance of Christ as *an ideal of man in the flesh* it has become as clear as day that the highest, final development of the person is precisely [. . .] so that man finds, realizes and believes with all the power of his nature that the highest use he can make of his person [. . .] is, as it were, to destroy this *I* and give it to all and to any without separation and without regret [. . .] So, on earth man strives for an ideal *opposite* to his nature. Whenever

man has failed to fulfill the law of striving for the ideal, that is, when he has not sacrificed in love his *I* to people or another being (Maria and I), he feels suffering and has named this state 'sin'. Thus, man should incessantly feel suffering which is balanced by the heavenly pleasure of fulfilling the law, that is, by sacrifice. This is earthly balance. Otherwise the earth would be meaningless.[25]

In the face of such personal trauma one might expect Dostoevsky to have behaved with more caution, but *Notes from Underground* shows how, out of the depths of dire necessity, Dostoevsky bet on a response of love.

The word 'notes' appears in the title or subtitle of all Dostoevsky's fictional works between 1859 and 1864, with the exception of 'Uncle's Dream'. In *The Village Stepanchikovo* and *The Insulted and the Injured* the genre of notes is associated with first-person fictional narratives. In *Notes from the Dead House* and *Winter Notes on Summer Impressions* it would appear to denote more the documentary character of the discourse. *Notes from Underground* combines both registers in an attempt to retain the tension between eternal questions and topical crises and to make sense of the chaotic life that surrounds the narrator without eviscerating it. A defining feature of these 'notes' is their narrators' mimicry of dominant ideological standpoints. (Throughout his life Dostoevsky was an accomplished impersonator and enthusiastic participant in amateur theatricals.) To a large degree all these 'notes' are more a visceral record of social disfiguration than an attempt to impose or even reveal an image.

The 'notes' also reflect the breakdown Dostoevsky perceived in the media system, without proposing any positive alternative. Dostoevsky's immersion in the mainstream media of his day was somewhat ironic given the price he had paid for his previous involvement in illicit networks of textual production, dissemination and performance. In the fictional works he wrote after returning to Petersburg Dostoevsky constantly highlighted the mechanisms of textual transmission and circulation. Prior to committing murder Raskolnikov calls attention to himself by publishing a newspaper article. The world of *Demons* is awash in illicit and inflammatory texts, both smuggled into Russia from abroad and printed domestically on underground printing presses, including Stavrogin's scandalous confession. Ivan Karamazov is the author of published and unpublished theological texts. Within the dense and fluid media sphere of Dostoevsky's novels the official press tends to produce more noise than understanding.[26]

The Underground Man constantly speaks in words borrowed from the contemporary media. The ideals against which he measures himself, and against which he then rebels, are imposed from without. He imagines how various scenarios will play out, only to realize that they are derivative of popular literary works. As Mikhail Bakhtin noted, his only path to freedom appears to lie in the 'destruction of [his] own image in [the other's] eyes, the sullying of that image [. . .] as an ultimate desperate attempt to free [himself] from the power of the other's consciousness'.[27] Only in his memory of Liza can he hear someone speaking to him as an individual, and only in response to her can he imagine himself saying something sincere, though his over-reflective consciousness prevents him from actually doing so. Only in such a private encounter could he reconcile himself to an open future, as opposed to the neat images of success that confront him at every turn from the public sphere. However, in the totalizing media world even this private encounter is tainted by the Underground Man's consciousness of its possible literary models and by his constant sense of shame, as if he is constantly being scrutinized by an audience; therefore he feigns haughty indifference and self-reliance. His final gesture shows him decisively choosing his projected, finalized identity over the more difficult restoration of emotional immediacy, which would require openness to the claims of the other. As Gary Saul Morson has remarked, 'Closure and structure mark the difference between life as it is lived and as it is read about; and real people live without the benefit of an outside perspective on which both closure and structure depend.'[28] The wall against which the Underground Man flails consists of words and images which he can never make his own.

The *Notes from Underground* powerfully affirm the unrealized potentialities within media culture and its ability to allow for unsightly reality to form itself into an image. In part one we see the Underground Man railing against a conventional wisdom derived from newspapers and journals, but instead of simply explaining his current state, the narrative of the second part also reveals points at which another kind of connection was possible between the Underground Man and others, especially Liza. This

A page from a Dostoevsky notebook, featuring a grotesque figure opposite a notation about the death of his first wife, *c.* 1864.

testimony to past possibility suffices to infuse the entire world with a new potentiality, and therefore with freedom. However, the Underground Man remains incapable of detaching his gaze from his immediate present, which is caught in webs of iron necessity. His inability to bring the story to a close prevents the notes from reaching any listeners who might hear him. The editor's decision to end the publication at Liza's departure, though the text goes on incessantly, marks a point where the story recedes before the enormity of a life – which can only be suggested, never captured, on the page.

In his editor's note to *Notes from Underground* Dostoevsky claims that the underground man is a necessary fiction: 'such persons as the writer of these notes not only may, but even must, exist in our society', he writes, but only as 'one of the representatives of a generation now coming to an end'.[29] An analogous formulation appears in the note 'From the Author' to *The Brothers Karamazov*, where Dostoevsky calls Alyosha an 'odd man' who nonetheless 'carries within himself the heart of the whole'.[30] However, unlike the earlier 'odd men', Alyosha represents a present that is open to a different future and bears within it all the unrealized potentialities of the past. These two prefaces describe the progress of Dostoevsky's imagination in the last twenty years of his life, from the Underground Man to the 'positively beautiful man', from the tyranny of the present to the as-yet-free future, and from the compulsive author to the responsive reader.

5

In Suspense

In mid-1865 Dostoevsky found himself back in the labour camp, figuratively speaking. The death in quick succession of his brother Mikhail and his wife Maria had left him in debt and alone, saddled with major new responsibilities for his brother's family and his hapless stepson Pavel. Throughout 1864 he had kept *Epokha* going by sheer force of will, scraping together loans, including 10,000 roubles from his aunt A. F. Kumanina, borrowed against his inheritance, and appealing for contributions to all sympathetic writers (and even the unsympathetic Ivan Turgenev). He went so far as to bond Apollon Grigoryev out of debtors' prison, only for Grigoryev to be incarcerated for another month before dying at the end of September. In this time Dostoevsky wrote practically nothing for himself, save the story 'The Crocodile' which shows that his rigorous analyses of contemporary society and politics or his personal travails had not dampened his riotous sense of humour.

On 14 April 1865 Dostoevsky wrote to Aleksandr Vrangel, his old friend from Semipalatinsk, to fill him in on his horrible year:

Would you believe it? The September issue [of *Epokha*] came out on 28 November, while the January issue for 1865 came out on 13 February, meaning that I spent sixteen days on each issue, each numbering 35 signatures [about 700 pages]. What this cost me! The main thing is that with all this forced hard labour I have been unable to write and publish in the journal a single line of my own. The public has not encountered my name, not even in Petersburg, let alone the provinces, [and] they don't know that I am editing the journal [. . .] I can't ascribe all this to poor management. After all it was I who began *Vremya*, not my brother, and *I* directed it and *I* edited it. In a word, we have experienced the same as an owner or a merchant whose house or factory has burnt down and who has turned from a wealthy man into a debtor.[1]

Everything he had achieved since returning to Petersburg had been endangered by a string of accidents. Clenched in this vice of necessity, Dostoevsky plotted his escape not through financial operations, but through literary experiment:

Now, in order to pay my debts, I want to publish my new novel in instalments, as is done in England. Moreover I want to publish *The Dead House* in instalments and with illustrations, as a deluxe edition, and then next year the full collection of my writings. All of this will yield about 15,000, but such forced labour it will be.

O, my friend, I would readily return to the forced labour camp for the same number of years to pay off my debts and feel free again. Now I am beginning to write my novel under the whip, I mean out of necessity, in a rush. It will be effective, but is this really what I need? Work out of necessity, out of a need for money, has crushed me and consumed me.[2]

In conclusion, Dostoevsky strikes a martial, even exuberant tone:

And yet for a beginning I need at least 3,000. I am looking in all corners to find this money, otherwise I shall perish. I sense that only luck can save me. From my entire reserves of strength and energy I have retained only something anxious and vague, something close to despair. Anxiety, grief, cold preoccupation, the most abnormal state for me, loneliness: what I had and who I was, as a 40-year-old, I no longer have. And yet I feel that I am only beginning to live. Funny, isn't it? Feline vivacity.[3]

This coy assertion echoes an observation he had once made about the resilience of the convicts he had lived among. He was one of them. He was a survivor.

Even as *Epokha* was collapsing around him Dostoevsky tried to remain optimistic, writing that he had shown himself to be 'not an entirely impractical man'.[4] Unfortunately his optimism was, as usual, exaggerated. After pushing through the second issue of *Epokha* for 1865, Dostoevsky faced up to the inevitable and closed the journal. Its subscribers were offered instead a nine-month subscription to *Biblioteka dlia chteniia*, the journal that had given the Dostoevsky brothers a taste for literature in the first place. Shot of the journal, if not of its debts, Dostoevsky set about resuming his literary endeavours, offering Kraevsky a novel entitled *The Drunkards*, which promised an analysis of alcoholism 'and all its extensions, mostly pictures of families, the education of children in this environment, etc. etc.'[5] Dostoevsky requested 3,000 roubles up front. Kraevsky declined. Facing debtors' prison, Dostoevsky was forced into a ruinous contract with the publisher Fyodor Stellovsky, whom the writer suspected of conspiring with his creditors to force him into a hole.

With this temporary reprieve, in mid-July Dostoevsky virtually fled to Wiesbaden. Western Europe represented for Dostoevsky a place where the usual limitations of his life were suspended, whether financial or creative. He justified his trip in typically rosy terms in a letter to Vrangel:

Both times I was abroad in [1862 and 1863] my health has resurrected with surprising speed. I promised to travel each year for three months, no more, especially since it has no financial consequence given the expense of life here. I wanted to travel to correct my health, to rest, recover, and work all the more easily during the remaining nine months of the year in Russia. But last year the death of my brother forced me to stay, and my current debts and activities are finishing me off for good. How I would want to travel for a month at least to air out my head, be refreshed, resurrect [. . . When] abroad I write constantly, because there is more time and peace there.[6]

The anticipated resurrection *ex machina* failed to transpire. By 10 August (by the Gregorian calendar) Dostoevsky had lost everything down to his watch. He resorted to sending humiliating pleas for loans to Alexander Herzen, Ivan Turgenev, his former lover Apollinaria Suslova, and even the local Orthodox priest Father Ioann Yanyshev (later a prominent theologian and pastor to the imperial court). It is not clear how often he saw Suslova at this time, but his letters to her are filled with stories of his mistreatment at the hands of hotel personnel who refuse to extend his credit: 'every day I leave the hotel at three and return at six to avoid giving the impression that I'm not having any dinner', he wrote on 24 August.[7] Unable even to afford a stamp, he reversed the charges when he wrote to Apollinaria Suslova: 'I try not even to think of myself; I sit and read, trying not to make myself hungry by moving.'[8] He returned to St Petersburg in October via Copenhagen, where he visited Vrangel, who gave Dostoevsky some cash and the winter coat off his back. Suslova also returned to Petersburg, where Dostoevsky insisted they marry and accused her of tormenting him in vengeance for the fact that she 'once gave herself' to him. Their relationship was nearing its end, however, and with it the entire cycle of humiliation it represented. Something new was beginning in Dostoevsky's life.

Though saddled with new debts and dressed in borrowed clothes, Dostoevsky returned to Petersburg with the beginnings of a novel that gave him new grounds for optimism. By the end of September he was proposing a much bolder plan to Mikhail Katkov (1818–1887), editor of the conservative Moscow journal *Russkii vestnik* (The Russian Messenger). Underlining how 'carried away' he was by the work, Dostoevsky wrote to Katkov: 'I vouch for its entertainment value, though I cannot judge its artistic merit myself.'[9] Now bearing the title *Crime and Punishment*, Dostoevsky's new novel commenced publication in *Russkii vestnik* at the new year. Despite his acute poverty, he delayed travelling to Moscow for the first instalments of his royalties, writing to Vrangel on 18 February 1866:

> I am waiting things out, and this is my goal: with God's help, this novel might be a most magnificent thing. I want at least three parts (that is, half of the entire novel) to be published, the effect will have been made among the public, and then I will go to Moscow and see whether they will try to lower my rate then. Quite the contrary, perhaps they will even increase it [. . .] Two weeks ago the first part of my novel came out in the first, January issue of *Russkii vestnik*. It is called *Crime and Punishment*. I have already heard many excited responses. There are bold and new things there.[10]

Emerging out of Dostoevsky's now-familiar atmosphere of oppression and rebellion, the novel *Crime and Punishment* would indeed elevate Dostoevsky's name to a wholly new status, becoming the most significant single factor in his enshrinement among the first rank of Russian and European writers – and the eventual amelioration of his material affairs.

But for the moment it was still just another long shot. Facing the impossibility of leaving for the summer, he wrote that 'the sad, disgusting and foul Petersburg in summer suits my mood and might even give me some false inspiration for the novel; but it's still too hard here'.[11] Unable to achieve the desired distance from his subject, Dostoevsky set about trying to combine the visceral effect of *Notes from the Dead House* and *Notes from Underground* with the kind of engaging narrative shape that had hitherto eluded him. The early plans for a novel about the social consequences of alcoholism remain wholly within the sentimental universe of *Poor Folk*, *Netochka Nezvanova* and *The Insulted and the Injured*, where downtrodden dreamers are locked in a tortuous cycle of pride and humiliation. One sees vestiges of the original conception in the subplot of the petty civil servant Marmeladov, whose daughter Sonya is forced into prostitution while he wallows in self-hatred. This subplot is, in a manner of speaking, timeless. Marmeladov is one of those poor who are always with us, who, like the Underground Man, has nowhere to go and remains nursing his sole possession: his own shame. Nothing decisive seems capable of happening to him. Living outside of time, he even thinks he can buy back his daughter's honour with a bit of money, if he could only save himself from spending it on drink. In *Crime and Punishment* this negative temporality clashes with the catastrophic temporality of Raskolnikov, who bursts open the closed cycle of necessity by taking an axe to the knot of despair.

Just as Dostoevsky bet on his own personal renewal in the act of writing the novel, the novel wagers on the resurrection of its main protagonist, with the ultimate hope for the resurrection of the reader and, through him, of society. These are extremely high ambitions for an artistic project. In almost every letter he wrote about the novel, Dostoevsky underscored the originality of the novel's intended form. To his friend Vrangel he wrote: 'By the end of November a lot was written and ready, but I burned it all; now I can own up to it. I didn't like it. A new form, a new plan carried me away, and I began from the beginning. I work day and night.'[12]

Even after this extensive planning, for the first time Dostoevsky was starting a narrative without a clear idea of how it would end. There are no epigraphs here, no guiding indications of the author's idea. He is like us, at the mercy of the very logic of the story as it develops in real time. But how could he be sure that the logic of this story would yield any mercy?

Dostoevsky was betting it would. In his letters to Mikhail Katkov, editor of *Russkii vestnik*, Dostoevsky stressed the topicality of his debunking of nihilistic tendencies among the youth. The urgency of the subject was especially evident when, on 4 April 1866, Dmitrii Karakozov (1840–1866) made an assassination attempt on Alexander II that bore a resemblance to Raskolnikov's crime. On 25 April 1866 Dostoevsky wrote to Katkov:

Speaking openly, I have been and think I shall always remain a real Slavophile according to my convictions [. . .] All nihilists are socialists. Socialism (especially in its Russian version) demands precisely the severing of all connections. They are completely convinced that on this *tabula rasa* they will immediately build paradise. Fourier, after all, was sure that one only needed to build a single phalanstery and the entire world would immediately be covered with phalansteries; these are his words. Our Chernyshevsky also said that he only needed to speak to the people for a half-hour and he would immediately convince them to convert to socialism. Our Russian boys and girls, so poor and defenseless, have their own eternal *main* point, which will be the basis of socialism for a long time to come, namely an enthusiasm for the good and the purity of their hearts. There are many swindlers and rascals among them. But all these schoolchildren and university students, of whom I have seen so many, have converted to nihilism so purely, so selflessly, in the name of honour, truth and true usefulness! Healthy science, of course, will wipe it out. But when might this occur?

How many victims will socialism consume before then? And, finally, healthy science, though it will take root, will not destroy the chaff so soon because healthy science is still science, not a direct form of civic and social activity.[13]

It is notable that, even in this context of acute ideological conflict, Dostoevsky insists on the good intentions of the youth and the need for a free press:

how can one fight nihilism without the freedom of speech? If they, the nihilists, were given the freedom of speech, then that might even work out advantageously: they would make all Russia laugh with the *positive* clarifications of their teaching. Whereas now they are given the semblance of Sphinxes, riddles, wisdom, mystery, and this tempts the naive.

Why shouldn't we even make investigations public, some ask? After all the chancellery might not even have anyone who could talk with the nihilists. Whereas here, in *glasnost'*, the entire society could help, and popular enthusiasm would not be absorbed by bureaucratic secrecy. This is seen as clumsiness, as the meekness of government measures, as an attachment to old forms.[14]

Dostoevsky wants to engage the nihilists in an open polemic and is confident of beating them on a level playing field. Raskolnikov is given ample opportunity to present his case before the reader. In fact, in *Crime and Punishment* Dostoevsky might be seen to be helping the nihilists to refine their arguments. (The French critic E.-M. de Vogüé attributed Karakozov's crime to a 'demon of imitation' that Dostoevsky awoke.[15]) For his part Dostoevsky was planning to utter a new word that would conquer on its own strength, not because of his growing alliance with structures of power.

After a quiet two months spent writing at a *dacha* outside Moscow, by October 1866 Dostoevsky once again fell victim to frequent epileptic attacks, exacerbated by the ominous approach of deadlines. Rarely has the word 'deadline' seemed more apt: under the terms of his contract with the publisher Stellovsky, Dostoevsky was obliged to submit both *Crime and Punishment* and a further novel by November 1866; in July of that year he was still mired in the first and had not even begun the second, aptly titled *The Gambler*. Should he fail to make it, he would be contractually obliged to give up all of his literary earnings for the next twenty years. On 17 June 1866 he wrote to a woman he was courting:

> I want to do an unprecedented and eccentric thing: to write in four months *thirty* signature leaves [*c.* 600 pages], in two different novels, of which one I shall write in the morning and the other in the evening, finishing both on deadline. Do you know, my dear Anna Vasilyevna, that up to now I've even enjoyed doing just such eccentric and extreme things. I am no good for the class of people who live solidly [. . .] I am convinced that not a single one of our writers, past and present, wrote in the conditions in which I continually write. Turgenev would perish from the very thought. But if you only knew how lamentable it is to ruin a thought that is being born within you when you know how good it is, and especially to be forced to ruin it on purpose![16]

As Dostoevsky ramped up the stakes of his artistic wager, he was in danger of compromising its artistic integrity.

Upon completing the novel, readers of *Crime and Punishment* face three major interpretive puzzles. First, there is the question of Raskolnikov's motivation for his double murder, for which several possibilities are presented without any one of them ever being marked as authoritative. The second puzzle is the way that Raskolnikov (and, indeed, other characters and even the narrator) dwell upon the pawnbroker as the main victim of his crime, wholly forgetting about his second, completely innocent victim, Lizaveta. Even at the very end of the novel, in prison, Raskolnikov continues to grapple with a reduced version of his crime that suggests his continuing moral blindness (or else a startling lapse of attention by the author). The third puzzle is the lack of satisfactory resolution at the end of the novel, particularly in the second chapter of the epilogue, which leaves us in suspense at the beginning of a 'new story, the story of a man's gradual renewal, the story of his gradual re-birth, his gradual crossing from one world into another'.[17]

Of the several motivations for the crime, most conspicuous is Raskolnikov's inclination to view himself as a new Napoleon, who, in Russian literature from Pushkin on, had become short-hand for Western-style individualism. This explanation featured in Dostoevsky's original conception. One of his plans reads:

The Idea of the Novel

1

The Orthodox View, What Orthodoxy Consists in

There is no happiness in comfort; happiness is bought for the price of suffering. Such is the law of our planet, but this immediate consciousness, sensed through the everyday process, is such a great joy that one can pay for it with years of suffering.

Man is not born for happiness. Man earns his happiness, and always through suffering.

There is no injustice here, for vital knowledge and consciousness (i.e., that which is felt immediately by the body and spirit, i.e. by the entire vital process) is acquired by experience *pro* and *contra*, which one must bear on oneself.

2

In his image the novel expresses the idea of immoderate pride, arrogance and contempt for this society. His idea: to take this society by force. Despotism is his characteristic. *She* goes counter to him.

NB: In the artistic execution don't forget that he is 23 years old.

He wants dominion but knows no means to this end. Immediately to take power and become rich. The idea of murder thus came to his mind.

NB: Whatever I might be, whatever I might do, – whether I am a benefactor of mankind or have sucked its living juices out of it like a spider, – is no business of mine. I know I want to rule, and that is enough.[18]

Much of this plan is evident in the novel. Raskolnikov's friend Razumikhin calls him a 'translation from a foreign tongue'.[19] However, Raskolnikov is much more complex than this sketch suggests, with a sadomasochism that combines 'Orthodox' suffering with Western 'dominion'; Razumikhin also accuses him of 'fussing over [his suffering] like a chicken with its egg'.[20] Moreover, within the novel Raskolnikov often presents his ideology with hesitation, almost apologetically, more as an excuse than as a conviction. The novel provides several more objective and plausible ways of explaining his actions. Tolstoy, in his later years as a moralizing bore, wrote that the crucial factor was Raskolnikov's indulgence in intoxicating substances. He could, of course, have been temporarily insane.

At the heart of all these explanations is the condition of poverty. The cycles of exchange and of violence are inscribed into one another, as are the cycles of pride and humiliation, of victimhood and victimization. By undermining faith in justice, systemic poverty leads directly to nihilism. Raskolnikov angrily concludes:

Man gets accustomed to everything, the scoundrel! [. . .]
But if that's a lie [. . .] if man in fact is not a scoundrel – in
general, that is, the whole human race – then the rest is all
mere prejudice, instilled fear, and there are no barriers, and
that's just as it should be!'[21]

On this reading *Crime and Punishment* is about a society caught
in the vice of forces of necessity, against which one misguided
but possibly noble young Prometheus has cause to revolt.

Another underlying cause is Raskolnikov's illusion of knowledge. Dostoevsky was consistently critical of scientific knowledge,
which can tell us only what is, not what can be; it can tell us much
about the laws of necessity, but absolutely nothing about what
humans actually choose to do. Scientific knowledge is 'a stick
with two ends', as Dostoevsky frequently wrote; it cuts both ways
and, giving no criterion for ethical judgement, can be directed to
whatever end. It is therefore, Dostoevsky felt, impossible to make
ethical conclusions from empirical observation and speculation.
The danger of ignoring the limits of knowledge is particularly
acute in modern societies where the density of information is so
great. Raskolnikov is quite susceptible to media influences, but his
attempts to engage in discourse tie him in knots. While in earlier
works the visual image sometimes seems to promise insight into
different potentialities in the world, in *Crime and Punishment* the
image remains mute and helpless, like the icons in the pawnbroker's
house which peer out helplessly upon the murders, and like the
icon to which Raskolnikov's mother prays without result.

Raskolnikov's inability to navigate his world is exacerbated
by his isolation from other people, which places him at the mercy
of others' ideas of him, at which he can only guess, leading to
paranoid fantasies. This oppressive isolation is underscored by the
cramped space of his garret, which is compared to a closed coffin.
Isolation mitigates Raskolnikov's kind impulses, for instance the

unaccountable charity which Raskolnikov directs at the Marmeladov family among others. His most forthrightly nihilistic statement comes right after he leaves a mound of change on the Marmeladovs' windowsill, an action he immediately regrets as irrational. Another glimpse of Raskolnikov's inherent goodness comes in his dreams and memories of childhood, but he appears to be almost violently resistant to their influence. Raskolnikov is intent to forget whence he came. This imprisons him – like the Underground Man – not only in the world of discourse, but also in the present moment, unable to construct a coherent story of his own identity.

A more capacious notion of Raskolnikov's condition, then, is that it is rooted in an erroneous understanding of time. Absent anywhere in Raskolnikov's calculations is the past. When he falls into unconsciousness the Russian word is 'oblivion' or, literally, 'memorylessness'. Accordingly his redemption would mean the recovery of memory, of his past, the binds of which enable and direct ethical action. As it is, without the grounding of a firm sense of his identity, instead of achieving the future he projects he is lost in the present, adrift of all temporal markers. He can only exert control over time by hastening its end.

Cast adrift in the present, buffeted by inhumane social forces, Raskolnikov ends up entrusting himself to chance. After all, his planning was propelled into action by an entire sequence of chance occurrences and coincidences, culminating in him overhearing Lizaveta promising to be somewhere else at seven o'clock. By relinquishing freedom over his own actions he succumbs to auto-matism, also to superstition, we are told, and the narrator comments that it was 'as though there were indeed some predestination, some indication in it'.[22] In the Russian these words ('*predopredelenie, ukazanie*') rhyme with the title of the novel (*Prestuplenie i nakazanie*), as if crime and punishment were somehow congruent with pre-destination and indication; by implication, ethical agency is always a contradiction of fate. No one is the author of his or her own life, but Raskolnikov has criminally ceded the power to narrate his life, that is, to shape it meaningfully. In order to do so Raskolnikov would need a stable viewpoint from which he can gain a fuller perspective on his actions. But it is not immediately evident that the novel would support this possibility.

Crime and Punishment is a doubled novel, the story of a double crime, a double punishment and a double reformation. Nowhere is Raskolnikov's submission to fate as evident as in his unanticipated and unpremeditated murder of Lizaveta, who wanders by chance into the apartment where her sister lies murdered, as the murderer lurks nearby:

> Seeing him run in, she began trembling like a leaf, with a faint quivering, and spasms ran across her whole face; she raised her

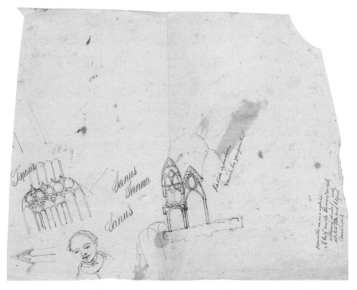

A manuscript page relating to *Crime and Punishment* featuring a portrait of Sonia and architectural details, *c.* 1865.

A page from a notebook relating to *Crime and Punishment*, c. 1865.

hand slightly, opened her mouth, but still did not scream and began slowly backing away from him into the corner, staring at him attentively, point-blank, but still not screaming, as if she was suffocating. He rushed at her with the axe; her lips became so pitifully distorted, as with very small children when they begin to be afraid of something, stare at the frightening object and prepare to scream [. . .] She merely brought her free left hand up, nowhere near her face, and slowly stretched it out towards him as if to keep him away.[23]

He brings the axe down on her and then makes his escape. If the murder of the pawnbroker was premeditated, this murder was caused solely on the force of circumstance.

When Raskolnikov murders the pawnbroker he removes the string around her neck, on which hangs a purse along with two crosses and a small icon; he drops the crosses on the woman's chest before going to seek out the pledges she kept. Her faith, we see, is intimately linked to her business; any redemption she could hope for was dependent upon her clients redeeming their tickets for the gold watches and other valuables they had committed as collateral.

In killing her Raskolnikov also rejects this faith and its relevance to his action. It is a gratuitous act, made as an expression of pure freedom. He quickly discards the valuables he steals; in any case the theft is a mere pretext to mislead the police. To the end of the novel he continues to deny that the murder of the pawnbroker was even a crime, let alone a sin. Even in the second epilogue, after his dream of nihilist society we are told: 'Everything, even his crime, even his sentence and exile, seemed to him now, in the first impulse, to be some strange, external fact, as if it had not even happened to him.'[24] This is because the pawnbroker's murder is still caught up in the dialectics of Raskolnikov's justifications, which have a modicum of logic, albeit of a fatally twisted variety. Words, Dostoevsky seems to be saying, can only get so far into the human conscience; dialectics must cede to life.

No such discursive explanation is available for Lizaveta's murder. Here it is not simply that Raskolnikov needs to accept ownership of the act in order to acknowledge responsibility for it; rather here he needs to discover the action itself, which he did not intend and which only faintly registered in his consciousness. Raskolnikov spends the first half of the novel finding his way back to Lizaveta. This is the overt role of Sonya, who was Lizaveta's friend and keeps Lizaveta's religious emblems, which were part of a gift-exchange with Sonya. The relationship between Sonya and Lizaveta raises the possibility of a community not based on an exchange of money and power. This is not love that has been merited; it is not based on whether the other person is worth loving, as demonstrated by Sonya's ability to love Raskolnikov. This unconditional love raises for Raskolnikov the possibility of a redemption not tied to a kind of financial logic of reparations, of a religion not based on a logic of power, and of a grace not linked to violence.

The crucial scene here is when Raskolnikov first comes to see Sonya and asks her to read the story of Lazarus to him from Lizaveta's New Testament.[25] He soon finds himself returning because, the narrator tells us, 'he *had* to tell her who killed Lizaveta'.[26] He does not know why he feels this need; perhaps it is in order to impress and gain power over Sonya. In any case, the inevitability of the moment returns him to the state of automatism in which he had killed:

> Again he covered his face with his hands and bent his head down. Suddenly he turned pale, got up from the chair, looked at Sonya, and, without saying anything, went mechanically and sat on her bed.
>
> This moment, as it felt to him, was frightfully similar to the one when he had stood behind the old woman, having already freed the axe from its hook, and realized that 'there was not another instant to lose'.[27]

He tells Sonya to guess who the murderer is:

> 'Take a good look'.
>
> As soon as he said this, a former, familiar sensation suddenly turned his soul to ice: he looked at her, and suddenly in her face he seemed to see the face of Lizaveta. He vividly recalled the expression of Lizaveta's face as he was approaching her with the axe and she was backing away from him towards the wall, her hand held out, with a completely childlike fright on her face, exactly as when little children suddenly begin to be frightened of something, stare fixedly and uneasily at the frightening object, back away, and, holding out a little hand, prepare to burst out crying. Almost the same thing now happened with Sonya as well: just as powerlessly, with the same fright, she looked at him for a time; then suddenly, holding out her left hand, she rested her fingers barely, lightly, on his chest, and slowly began to get up from the bed, backing farther and farther away from him, while her gaze at him

became ever more immobile. Her terror suddenly communicated itself to him: exactly the same fright showed on his face as well; he began looking at her in exactly the same way, and even with almost the same *childlike* smile.[28]

If the first time Raskolnikov murdered Lizaveta it was mechanical, forced by the logic of predestination, then the second time it becomes a matter of freedom. He becomes afraid of himself because he sees himself, the child who once tried to intercede to save a horse, as an executioner.

Sonya's role in the novel is contrasted to that of the detective, Porfiry Petrovich, Raskolnikov's other confessor. Porfiry is a very smart policeman, but he is still a policeman who works within relatively rigid conceptions of cause and effect. He recognizes that the murder of the pawnbroker follows the logic presented in Raskolnikov's ill-fated newspaper article. He follows these clues and identifies a main suspect. Lizaveta hardly enters into his considerations at all; she was obviously an accident. But then he is also unable to find secure knowledge of the crime. As he says, both human psychology and circumstantial evidence cut both ways; they point to possibilities, but never to certainties. Porfiry has mastered the web of necessary causes that could lead a man like Raskolnikov to murder a pawnbroker. However, without access to the realm of freedom he remains incapable of understanding *why* Raskolnikov chose to do so. Nor, indeed, can Raskolnikov understand himself on such terms.

In her interrogations Sonya does not use sly, provocative discourse; rather she looks at Raskolnikov and renders herself physically present to him. Some of the most eloquent exchanges between the two are when they sit together for some minutes in silence, as she waits for him to speak. When he hesitates at the police station it is her silent gaze that sends him back in to complete his confession. The exchange of gazes is given material form in the exchange of religious objects. When Sonya first offers him her cross, saying that she will wear Lizaveta's, he is not yet ready to accept it. Only later does he return 'for her crosses'; as he puts it:

> O, this is a symbol of my taking a cross upon myself, heh, heh! That's right, I haven't suffered enough yet! Cypress, for simple folk; the brass one, Lizaveta's, you're keeping for yourself – can I see it? So she was wearing it . . . at that moment? I also know of two similar crosses, a silver one and a little icon. I let them drop on the old crone's chest that time. It would really be more to the point if I put those on now.[29]

Rejecting the option of suicide on a bridge standing over a river, he crosses himself, goes to the crossroads, and confesses, albeit only on the second try: 'It was I who killed the official's old widow and her sister Lizaveta with an axe and robbed them.'[30] It is characteristic of him that he can only claim ownership of his actions when he places himself at the centre of the cross, his actions overdetermined by the self-sacrificial role he is playing. In this light the Epilogue becomes more conclusive. Even if he cannot quite persuade himself to set aside his dialectics, he has begun to love Sonya, and this very gift of unconditional love is a form of repentance: that is, both a punishment and a liberation.

As he proceeded with the project Dostoevsky came to see that what he could present was not really a *word*, which would get caught up in dialectics just like Raskolnikov's casuistry. Nor was it an *image*, which might gaze silently onto the other characters, like the novel's meek icons. What he discovered here is the idea of artistic form as a kind of *way*, one for which there was no map, no model. The originality of the novel's form, which Dostoevsky asserted in almost every statement about it, is in the combination of onward-driving suspense structures and suspended metaphysical horizons. The unity of this suspense and the suspension is visible and palpable in the extended gestures that fill the novel, moments that are both culminating and pregnant with possibility. *Crime and Punishment* was a breakthrough novel for Dostoevsky because here for the first time aesthetic form enacts its own social and metaphysical ramifications.

At the beginning of October 1866 Dostoevsky set aside his work on *Crime and Punishment*, prolonging the torment of readers who were hanging on each monthly instalment, awaiting the 'punishment' promised in the title. To meet his contractual obligations Dostoevsky had to produce a new novel by 1 November. To meet this obligation he hired a young stenography student, Anna Grigoryevna Snitkina, and set about dictating a novel according to a plan he had worked out, based on the catastrophic bout of gambling and erotic passion he had experienced in 1865. Set in the fictional German town of Roulettenburg, the epitome of modern rootlessness and superficiality, *The Gambler* tells of Aleksei, who works for a Russian noble family as teacher of their children. Surrounded by bourgeois calculations of risk and profit, he creates for himself an erotic, even mystical religion of pure chance, based on the worship of Lady Luck. The result is at once the apotheosis and the collapse of modern Western value systems. Gary Saul Morson has said that Aleksei's theological 'mistake is to try to compel what can only be had as a divine gift'.[31] Morson finds no positive 'moral' to be derived from the novel. From Dostoevsky's perspective, it was intended to have a positive (perhaps even cathartic) *effect* on readers by involving them in a wounding spiral of passion and despair.

Suspense draws readers through the narrative, structuring the temporality of the events. It is the engine of the work's effect on readers. Walter Benjamin saw suspense in a negative light, as a crucial element in the capitalist economy of modern fiction, which is consumed like any other disposable product: 'The suspense which permeates the novel is very much like the draft which stimulates the flame in the fireplace and enlivens its play.'[32] In his brutal analysis of Balzac's story 'Sarrasine', Roland Barthes described the drive to get to the end and solve enigmas as a concealment of the failures inherent to language and narrative. To these 'readerly' or 'classic' texts Barthes opposed 'writerly' ones marked by suspension, where language, imagery and narrative collapse before the unutterable truths they contemplate. This halting makes audible the inverted voice of the text, distinct from that of its author: 'What sings, what flows smoothly, what moves by accidentals, arabesques and controlled ritardandos through an intelligible progression (like the melody often given the woodwinds) is the series of enigmas, their suspended disclosure, their delayed resolution.'[33] When this voice becomes dominant, the narrative gradually forms itself into a suspended, 'pensive' text:

> Just as the pensiveness of a face signals that this head is heavy with unspoken language, so the (classic) text inscribes within its system of signs the signature of its plenitude: like the face, the text becomes *expressive* (let us say that it signifies its expressivity), endowed with an interiority whose supposed depth compensates for the parsimony of its plural. At its discreet urging, we want to ask the classic text: *What are you thinking about?* but the text, wilier than all those who try to escape by answering: *about nothing,* does not reply, giving meaning its last closure: suspension.[34]

Dostoevsky's fiction shows that, far from an either/or proposition, suspense and suspension are always locked in mutual dependence. (Notably, the meanings coincide in the French term *suspension*.) The forward and outward thrust of Dostoevsky's fictions remains dependent upon the tension of each suspended moment. Their infinite lateral expansion into the world is propelled by the pulsating instants of execution time.

Dostoevsky began as a playwright and remained fascinated with the medium throughout his life, as one sees in the description of prison theatricals in *Notes from the Dead House* and from his frequent public readings later in life. He even played parts in amateur shows, including a presentation of Pushkin's *Stone Guest* in 1880. However, he was ambivalent about the attempts made to stage his fictional works during his lifetime, which he regarded as insufficiently bold in re-imagining the fictions for the different medium. In 1872 Dostoevsky responded to a correspondent who proposed making *Crime and Punishment* into a drama:

> There is some secret of art, according to which the epic form will never find its correlation in dramatic form. I even believe that for various forms of art there exist corresponding series of poetic ideas, so that one idea can never be expressed in another form that does not correspond to it.
>
> It's another matter if you re-do and change the novel as much as possible, preserving from it one mere episode, in order to re-work it as a drama, or, taking the original idea, completely change the plot?[35]

Dostoevsky's narrative fictions of suspense have often been most successfully adapted in other media by means of their radical suspension. The Soviet artist Lev Bruni thought that, formally, *The Adolescent* was a verbal Parthenon, an opinion which his friend Nikolai Punin found incomprehensible.[36] Proust was on firmer ground (in *The Captive*) when he compared *The Brothers Karamazov* to a architectural frieze, proceeding from the first episode of Smerdyakov's birth to the murder of Fyodor Pavlovich and, eventually, Smerdyakov's suicide.[37] Fernand Léger expressed his fascination with Dostoevsky's technique of 'personification through enlarged detail, the individualization of the fragment, where the drama begins, is set, and stirs', a technique that overturns 'the scale of ordinary and conventional values' and that points to a 'cinema of the future'.[38]

Indeed, the most adventurous adaptations of Dostoevsky have been in the cinema. Using the murder of the pawnbroker from *Crime and Punishment* (and wholly ignoring Lizaveta), Sergei Eisenstein surprised his students by insisting on a stationary camera, a choice that struck them as 'un-cinematic'. Keeping the camera still demonstrates how to utilize subtle matters of *mise en scène*, character position, angle, scale and camera optics: 'for every scene of action you make your own special field'.[39] The result, Karla Oehler remarks, is a 'drama of scale' that captures within the frame the entire dialectic of Raskolnikov's Napoleonic dreams and microbial nightmares.[40] This same fascination with Dostoevsky's *mises en scène* is evident in a list by Andrei Tarkovsky of twelve scenes around which he would base his planned adaptation of *The Idiot* 'on a small, intimate scale'.[41] Tarkovsky left a detailed account of how he would shoot the novel's climactic scene:

> What overwhelming truth in their characters and circumstances! As Rogozhin and Myshkin, their knees touching, sit there on chairs in that enormous room, they astound us by the combination of an outwardly absurd and senseless *mise en scène* with the perfect veracity of their own inner state [. . .] Here the *mise en scène* arises out of the psychological state of particular characters at a particular moment, as a unique statement of the complexity of their relationship. The director, then, to build up a *mise en scène*, must work from the psychological state of the characters, through the inner dynamic of the mood of the situation, and bring it all back to the truth of the one, directly observed fact, and its unique texture.[42]

Tarkovsky never did make his adaptation of *The Idiot*, though *Sacrifice* (1986) comes so close that its protagonist Alexander is once even addressed as 'Myshkin'. One imagines, though, that he could have made an entire full-length film out of a very limited number of scenes, or even out of this one scene (which contains long periods of silence, like Sonya's conversations with Raskolnikov). One gets a sense of how Tarkovsky's film might have looked from Aleksandr Sokurov's 1992 film *Whispering Pages*, subtitled 'on motifs from classical Russian literature', which in lieu of the story provides a study in the optical atmospheres of *Crime and Punishment,* particularly its claustrophobic *mises en scène* and the desperate, pointless violence that pervades the characters' interactions.

The filmmaker who has developed the closest creative dialogue with Dostoevsky was undoubtedly Robert Bresson. Dostoevskian motifs are prominent throughout Bresson's oeuvre, from *A Man Escaped* (1956) to *L'Argent* (1983), but Bresson presented three pictures as formal adaptations of Dostoevsky's fictions: *Pickpocket* (1959), *A Gentle Creature* (*Une femme douce*, 1969) and *Four Nights*

Whispering Pages, dir. Aleksandr Sokurov, 1992, film still.

Pickpocket, dir. Robert Bresson, 1959, film still.

of a Dreamer (*Quatre nuits d'un rêveur*, 1971). In each case, Bresson ascetically empties the *mise en scène* of all conspicuous dramatic elements, focusing in on individual details and gestures. It is as if he has used not the final text, but rather Dostoevsky's drafts, replete with the obsessive doodles of faces and windows. In his *Notes on the Cinematographer*, Bresson remarked:

> Proust says that Dostoevsky is original in composition above all.
> It is an extraordinarily complex and close-meshed whole, purely
> inward, with currents and counter-currents like those of the sea,
> a thing that is found also in Proust (in other ways so different)
> and whose equivalent would go well with a film.[43]

Bresson explained: 'If I make a film from Dostoevsky, I try always to *take out* all the literary parts. I try to go directly to the sentiments of the author and only what can pass through me.'[44]

The effect of this filtering is to achieve in cinema the kind of open form of Dostoevsky's fictions, which, as Brian Price has demonstrated in remarkable detail, allowed both Bresson and Dostoevsky to respond with acute sensitivity to their historical moments, sculpting tensile forms of violent saturation only to set off those spaces – those silences – in which a healing presence – grace, or freedom, perhaps – becomes palpably though elusively manifest.[45]

The most compelling philosophical account of how Dostoevsky made fictional form into such a potent metaphysical machine is given by Jean-Paul Sartre in his essay 'Why Write?' For Sartre, the final goal of art is 'to recover this world by giving it to be seen as it is, but as if it had its source in human freedom'.[46] The first part of the task necessarily involves the reader as co-creator, since it is only the reader's subjective engagement that grants the narrative objective, temporal form. Suspense is a crucial means of eliciting the reader's affective involvement in the construction of the fictional world:

> Without waiting, without a future, without ignorance, there is no objectivity [. . .] Raskolnikov's waiting is *my* waiting which I lend him. Without this impatience of the reader he would remain only a collection of signs [. . .] it is not [Raskolnikov's] behaviour which excites my indignation or esteem, but my indignation and esteem which give consistency and objectivity to his behaviour.[47]

However, to become engaged in a narrative is not to end up in its thrall, as Benjamin and Barthes would have it. Rather, the second part of Sartre's definition requires that the reader's response be free and sincere, outside of 'the chain of determinism'.[48] The author 'present[s] the world to [. . .] freedoms' in 'an act of confidence in the freedom of men'.[49] Insofar as it is imaginary the reader's freedom remains in suspension, but the end of the fiction releases the reader back into a world that now awaits his free action. Sartre goes so far as to say that 'The art of prose is bound up with the only regime in which prose has meaning, democracy.'[50] It is a thought that has more recently been extended by Giorgio Agamben apropos of Martin Heidegger:

> By transforming the principle of man's delay before truth into a poetic process and renouncing the guarantees of truth for love of transmissibility, art succeeds once again in transforming man's inability to exit his historical status, perennially suspended in the inter-world between old and new, past and future, into the very space in which he can take the original measure of his dwelling in the present and recover each time the meaning of his action.[51]

The interdependence of suspense and suspension in Dostoevsky's fictional world, as the means by which the reader first enters and then exits the fictional realm into a transformed reality, testifies to the possibility of freedom in the shadow of the Dead House.

6

Dreams and Demons

Dostoevsky's exploits of 1866 not only precipitated a revolution in fiction; they also put him onto a much firmer footing in his life and career. Though he remained heavily in debt, he had successfully met the conditions of his contract with the publisher Stellovsky and, with *Crime and Punishment* a major success, could anticipate lucrative new editions and contracts. In early 1867 he married the young stenographer Anna Grigoryevna Snitkina (1846–1918), who had enabled him to complete *The Gambler* on time. Energetic and efficient, Anna brought Dostoevsky much-needed stability and joy in his home life. Twenty-five years his junior, at first she fought an unequal battle against Dostoevsky's worst habits, like his gambling. Over time, however, she proved to be a formidable force in her own right.

The newlyweds immediately departed St Petersburg for Western Europe, where they would remain for four and a half lonely years. Dostoevky was as far from his readers as he was from his creditors, working tirelessly to build on the breakthrough of *Crime and Punishment* and earn enough money for a safe return. Europe meant many things to him. For one thing, he found himself free to meet with political émigrés and follow ideological debates without the restrictions of Russian government censorship. In addition to reading the Russian émigré press, especially Alexander Herzen's journal *Kolokol* (The Bell), in 1867 Dostoevsky attended sessions of the Congress for Peace and Freedom in Geneva, taking in speeches

Unknown photographer, *Anna Grigoryevna Dostoevskaya*, c. 1871.

by leaders of the international Left (though not the anarchist Mikhail Bakunin, whose speech he read in the press); in a letter to his old friend Apollon Maikov he described it as 'four days of screaming and cursing'.[1] Perhaps reminded of his own radical youth, he set to work on a memoir of Belinsky, which unfortunately has been lost.

More important than this political liberty, though, was the liberating distance between him and the binds of family and finance. Europe encouraged wagers, in fiction as in the casinos (to which Dostoevsky continued to make periodic visits when money was short, invariably with disastrous results) and thus was a place that encouraged an imaginative re-engagement with Russian life. Dostoevsky later described his life in Dresden to his friend Maikov:

> why am I in Dresden, in Dresden of all places, and not some-where else, and why was it worth leaving everything in one place and moving to another? The answer was clear (my health, my debts, etc.), but it was awful that I felt that wherever I might live it is *all the same*: whether Dresden or elsewhere, it is all a foreign country, everywhere a stranger's crust of bread. I wanted to get right down to work but I felt that I could not work at all, it was not the right impression at all. What did I do? I idled. I read, wrote a bit, suffered from boredom and then from the heat. The days passed monotonously. Anya and I regularly walked in the Great Park after dinner, listened to cheap music, then read, then went to sleep.[2]

The matriarch of the Epanchin family captures this paradoxical attraction to and repulsion from Europe in the closing line of *The Idiot*: 'all this life abroad, and all this Europe of yours, is all a fantasy; and all of us, when we're abroad, we are also mere fantasy . . .'[3]

Dostoevsky's fantasy of Europe was closely linked to the paintings he found in its museums. In Dresden he discovered Claude Lorrain's mythic landscape *Acis and Galatea* (1657), which impressed him as capturing the paradisal childhood of humanity, at least of Western civilization. In the dreams of the venal noble-man Versilov in Dostoevsky's novel *The Adolescent*, this image of the 'setting sun of the first day of European humanity' becomes an apocalyptic vision of 'the last day of European humanity', accompanied by its death knoll and filled with references to the Franco–Prussian War of 1871, which Dostoevsky followed closely while abroad.[4] Versilov is consoled only by his ability to imagine a new dawn for humanity, arising from a new generation of humans: 'Europe has created the noble types of the Frenchman, Englishman and German, but it knows next to nothing about its own future man.'[5] Versilov identifies this 'future man' with the Russian, but in the story 'The Dream of a Ridiculous Man', part of Dostoevsky's

Raphael's *Sistine Madonna*, 1512–13, today in the Staatliche Kunstsammlungen, Dresden.

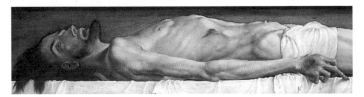

A detail of Hans Holbein's *The Body of the Dead Christ in the Tomb*, 1521–2, today in the Kunstmuseum, Basel.

Writer's Diary for 1877, a similar scenario of fall and regeneration plays out within the conscience of a single modern individual.

Dresden also opened Dostoevsky's eyes to Raphael's *Sistine Madonna*, which for him possessed the quality not of a beginning or ending, but of timeless beauty. On 27 June 1867 Anna Dostoevskaya noted in her diary:

> As usual Fedya doesn't like anything today [. . .] This usually happens to him when all his impressions change after an [epilectic] attack. Fedya can never get a good look at the *Sistine Madonna* because he can't see so far and he doesn't have a pince-nez. Today for instance it occurred to him to stand on a chair before the *Madonna* in order to get a closer look at it [. . .] A guard came up to Fedya and told him it was not allowed.[6]

Given a framed photographic copy by the philosopher Vladimir Solovyov, Dostoevsky hung the Sistine Madonna in his study. The painting is mentioned in all of his mature novels except for *The Brothers Karamazov*. More often than not, however, it represents a supine beauty that is helpless before the world's violence and cynicism.

After a ruinous sojourn in Baden-Baden, frittered away at the city's roulette tables and pawnshops, the Dostoevskys moved to Geneva, where on 5 March 1868 Anna Grigoryevna gave birth to a daughter, Sophia. Dostoevsky lovingly described her to Maikov:

'The child is only a month old but has my complete facial expression, my complete physiognomy, right down to the wrinkles on my forehead; she lies there as if she's composing a novel!'[7] On the way to Geneva they stopped off in Basel with the express purpose of seeing Hans Holbein the Younger's *The Body of the Dead Christ in the Tomb* (1521–2), the effect of which was recounted by Anna: 'The picture made an overwhelming impression on Fyodor Mikhailovich; he stopped before it as if in shock. [. . .] His agitated face showed the kind of frightened expression which I repeatedly had occasion to observe in the first moments of an epileptic fit.'[8] If Claude Lorrain and Raphael represented for Dostoevsky the power of Western art to create and sustain a life world, then Holbein's painting testified to the ways in which contemporary Western civilization was intently killing God off. In *The Idiot* Holbein's painting hangs in the house of the murderer Rogozhin as if to assert a direct relation between the death of God and the protagonists' struggle with a hostile world. As Ippolit describes it:

this is a man's corpse in the fullest form, having suffered endless torments even before being nailed to the cross [. . .] One unwittingly thinks that, if death is frightful and the laws of nature so strong, how can one overcome them? [. . .] When one looks at this painting nature appears to one in the form of an enormous, implacable and mute beast, or rather, strange as it might seem, in the form of some kind of enormous machine of the newest construction, which has senselessly seized, crushed and consumed, without regard and without feeling, a great and priceless being.[9]

Holbein's painting haunted Dostoevsky by neutralizing the possibility of resurrection, which was for Dostoevsky the sole pledge of merciful liberation from the forces of necessity. It is no wonder that the mortally ill Ippolit bequeaths his skeleton to

This contemporary photograph of Dostoevsky's final apartment in St Petersburg (now the Dostoevsky Museum) shows a reproduction of Raphael's *Sistine Madonna* given to Dostoevsky by Vladimir Solovyov.

'science' and, at the same time, consoles himself with a curious notion of immortality: 'A dead man has no age, you know.'[10] At the same time, Holbein's annihilating image sharpened for Dostoevsky the wager of faith: if *this* smouldering body was capable of holding such a 'great and priceless being – a being who alone was worth all of nature and all its laws', then there is hope for our own sordid world. Such ethereal visions as Lorrain's *Acis and Galatea* and Raphael's *Sistine Madonna*, which provide healing images not yet corrupted by violence, could no longer overcome the material challenge of Holbein's image. That required a new physiology of art.

By the end of 1868 the Dostoevskys had moved onto Florence, via Milan, driven back onto the road by the death of Sophia in May 1868. Despite the despair of losing a child, along the way Dostoevsky penned a humourous poem describing his current plight:

> We've lived for two years in poverty,
> We have only our clear conscience,
> From Katkov we're waiting for royalties
> For a novel that is sheer nonsense.
> Where's your conscience, o brother?
> You promised *The Dawn* a novel,
> You've got an advance from Katkov,
> And promised a story to send off.
> You've wasted your last pfennig
> On the roulette tables of Europe,
> And now not even a penny
> Do you have to your name, you ninny![11]

Again Dostoevsky charted his peregrinations at least in part by the art works on display in local picture galleries. Their return to Dresden in July 1869 was stimulated no less by Dostoevsky's desire to return to his beloved *Madonna*, than by considerations of climate (Anna was pregnant again). They stayed in Dresden until they were finally able to return to Petersburg in July 1871.

Suspended between the depression of exile and the elation of unbridled fantasy, Dostoevsky proceeded to plan out the continuation of the project he had begun with *Crime and Punishment*. He would use his distance from Russia to analyse the forces pervading its social structures, from individual couples up to entire cities. He would plot these forces as leading to critical moments of catastrophe and revelation, using the devices of the literary thriller to foreground the metaphysical dimensions of contemporary concerns. And amid the collision of these forces of necessity he would seek out spaces and faces through which a redemptive grace might emerge from within a barren world.

In addition to its innovative narrative structure and characterization, which allowed Dostoevsky to marry stark realism to metaphysical mystery, *Crime and Punishment* established a working method that Dostoevsky would rely on for each of his four remaining novels. In each case he spent the better part of a year reading, charting out endless plans for the plot and key scenes, sketching characters' faces and negotiating terms with a journal (usually *Russkii vestnik*). At the turn of the new year he launched himself into an extended bout of writing, submitting monthly instalments to the journal, adjusting his plans as needed and haggling for advances and extensions until he finished in exhaustion, usually a month or two behind schedule, at the beginning of the third year. Dostoevsky kept wildly irregular hours, often working through the night and rising only for a late lunch. Armed with his notes, at times he continued to dictate the text to Anna. Over the four-plus years of European exile Dostoevsky used this method to write the novels *The Idiot* and *Demons*, as well as the novella *The Eternal Husband*. The extensive working plans and notes give fascinating insights into Dostoevsky's interests and thoughts, as well as into the origins of characters and scenes in the novels; they must be used with great care, however, since Dostoevsky's craftsman-like shaping of his narratives invariably transformed the composite elements into something he had not entirely foreseen.

The end of 1867 had arrived before Dostoevsky felt ready to start writing *The Idiot* – the 'unsuccessful novel' mentioned in his ditty. On 31 December he wrote to Apollon Maikov:

> Overall the plan has come together. From here on out only the details gleam, tempting me and feeding my flame. But the whole? But the protagonist? Because the whole emerges for me in the form of the protagonist. Thus it has worked for me. I must establish the image. Will he develop under my pen? [. . .] Of the four protagonists two have been traced solidly *in my soul*, one is yet to be traced at all, and the fourth, i.e. the main protagonist, [. . .] is extremely weak. Maybe he doesn't sit so weakly in my heart, but he is frightfully difficult.[12]

By the end of January 1868 the first instalment had been published in *Russkii vestnik*, and the novel continued to appear on a monthly basis for the next year, with the final chapters reaching subscribers (in a special supplement) in March 1869. He never did get the face of the main protagonist quite right, however, perhaps because it was too close to his heart.

The plot of *The Idiot* is difficult to summarize because so little actually occurs outside of the protagonists' minds. Prince Myshkin, who has suffered all his life from epilepsy and other, less well-defined ailments, returns to Petersburg from a Swiss sanatorium. He has only 25 roubles to his name, but he soon connects with distant relatives (the Epanchin family) and their circle; he also receives an inheritance that makes him a plausible, if not especially advantageous match for Aglaya, the youngest of the

Epanchins' three daughters. However he also falls prey to the stunning beauty and mysterious charms of Nastasya Filippovna Barashkova, whose many paramours include the suspicious Parfyon Rogozhin. Buffetted by his own contradictory desires and others' manipulations, Myshkin abandons Aglaya and almost marries Nastasya Filippovna, only for her to be stolen away at the last minute by Rogozhin, who stabs her to death. Myshkin ends the novel back at Dr Schneider's Swiss sanatorium, in something close to a catatonic state.

This story of family, friendship and erotic love might seem like a 'potpourri of Italian operas', but its internal workings continually open up onto much broader horizons.[13] The plot is propelled by rumours, suspicions, secrets, lies, notes and public scandals, all of which call into question the mechanics by which we gain knowledge of the other – or, indeed, of ourselves. Dostoevsky asks whether such knowledge can ever come in the form of information, or whether one must rely on what can only be called revelation, which is what Prince Myshkin seems to draw on in moments of vision that accompany his epileptic fits:

> These instants were nothing other than an amplification of self-consciousness, – if one has to express this state with a single word, – self-consciousness and, at the same time, self-sensation (of a supremely direct nature) [. . .] 'At this moment', as he once told Rogozhin in Moscow, during their meetings there, 'at this moment I suddenly understand the unusual words that *time will be no more*.'[14]

It seems that one can only know oneself in instants of apocalypse, such as those (the reader is repeatedly told) preceding execution, when linear time expands into other dimensions.

This apocalyptic horizon is invoked repeatedly throughout the novel, both in connection to Myshkin's intimations of timelessness

A page from a notebook for *The Idiot*, *c.* 1867, featuring an early sketch by Dostoevsky of the titular character.

and also, disconcertingly, with the character of Lukyan Lebedev, a scoundrel and inveterate liar. He claims to be a specialist in the interpretation of St John's Book of Revelation, a 'professor of the Antichrist'.[15] He has instructed Nastasya Filippovna ('a lady with an agitated imagination, hee-hee!') in the matter: 'She agreed with me that we are in the era of the third horse, the black one, and in the era of the horseman who holds a pair of scales in his hand, since everything in our age is based on the measure and the contract, and everyone is seeking his rightful share.'[16] According to his interpretation of Revelation 8:10-11, the '"star Wormwood" in the Apocalypse, which falls to earth onto the source of the waters, is [. . .] the web of railways that has covered Europe.'[17] Against this metaphysical backdrop, however, it is the devil, not God, who commands belief: 'Do you know who the devil is?', Lebedev asks. 'Do you know his name? And without even knowing his name you laugh at his form, following Voltaire's example, at his hooves, tail and horns, which you yourselves have invented; for the impure spirit is a great and awesome spirit, not with the hooves and horns which you have invented for him.'[18] This literally disfigured devil reappears as the spider in the claustrophobic nightmare which the consumptive Ippolit relates in his 'Necessary Explanation' of his 'final conviction', and about which he asks: 'Can one dream an image of that which has no image?'[19] This horror of being unsighted – linked to the horror of seeing a dead God in Holbein's painting – leads Ippolit to revolt against his own birth, presaging Ivan Karamazov's similar rebellion in Dostoevsky's final novel.[20]

Instead of projecting a healing image, then, *The Idiot* mercilessly questions the possibility of an image that could yield mercy and grace. Compared to the scenes in *Crime and Punishment* where Raskolnikov and Sonya engage in silent communication, there is a striking ambivalence to Myshkin's suspended moments, such as when, on the verge of a fit, Myshkin is joined by a 'strange and frightful demon':

> was there really something in Rogozhin, that is, in the entire *current* image of this man, in the entire aggregate of his words, movements, actions, views, that could justify the prince's frightful portents and his demon's disturbing whisperings? Something that is seen automatically, but which is difficult to analyse and relate, which is impossible to justify with sufficient reason, but which still makes, despite all this difficulty and impossibility, a perfectly integral and indelible impression, that unwittingly passes into a full conviction?[21]

Expressed in the horrific face of Myshkin as he enters into his epileptic fit, this 'conviction' is communicated to Rogozhin as 'an impression of sudden terror' which freezes Rogozhin in his tracks and 'save[s] the prince from the inevitable blow of the knife which was already falling onto him'.[22] The image can avert a crime, but it is helpless against the evil.

The Idiot is the novel that reveals most about Dostoevsky's inner life, his experience as an epileptic and his dreams of (and for) his world. He gave Prince Myshkin one of his own recurrent dreams, in which he defeats Austrian forces in a glorious military campaign. More prominent, of course, are the nightmares, like Ippolit's vision of the tarantula. The playful Russian writer Aleksei Remizov (1877–1957), who devoted many inspired pages to the interpretation of dreams in nineteenth-century Russian fiction, wrote that the entire fourth book is a dream that begins when Nastasya Filippovna appears before Myshkin as a 'vision' at the entrance of the park in Pavlovsk.[23] Certainly the final scene, set in the twilight of a Petersburg white night, when Myshkin silently consoles the murderer of his bride, has all the intensity and obscurity of a life-changing dream.

Seen as the 'new story' which Dostoevsky promised in the epilogue to *Crime and Punishment*, *The Idiot* is frequently read as the first return on Dostoevsky's desire 'to represent a positively beautiful man. More difficult than this', he wrote to his cousin Sophia Ivanova on New Year's Day 1868, 'there is nothing in the world, especially now'.[24] Accordingly, Myshkin has often been seen as a Christ-figure, too good for the world around him, too honest for human relationships. For all his prophetic revelations, insights and dreams, however, Myshkin remains helpless to act, incapable of producing an effect in the physical world: 'I don't possess a seemly gesture, a feeling of measure', he confesses early on.[25] When he accidentally makes a 'grand gesture', he ruins his pre-engagement party with Aglaya by knocking over a priceless vase, making intemperate speeches about Catholicism and causing general embarrassment.[26] His perception of the world is also curiously immaterial. He falls in love with Nastasya Filippovna via her photographic portrait, and her face remains a terrifying cipher for him throughout the novel. The narrator remarks that Myshkin also looked upon Aglaya 'like an object located a mile away from him, or like a portrait, not the real her'.[27] She responds that she is afraid that 'you want to reach out your hand and touch my face with your finger, so as to feel it'. This is similar to the gesture with which Myshkin consoles the murderer Rogozhin: 'The prince sat alongside him motionlessly on the mat and, at every explosion of the sick man's cries or delirium, hurried to draw his trembling hand across his hair and cheeks, as if to caress and pacify him.'[28] With these tentative gestures – those of a 'stranger' to the world – Myshkin seems less like Christ than like doubting Thomas, unable to turn conviction into action.[29] In the aftermath of his 'grand gesture' Myshkin is even suspected of nihilism.

The mood at the end of the novel is indeed reminiscent of the suspense felt by Christ's disciples after the death, but before seeing proof of resurrection. Sitting with the insensate Myshkin alongside her body, Rogozhin senses the odour of death setting in. The reader recalls that nearby there hangs Holbein's painting, which had led Ippolit to wonder how the disciples 'could believe, seeing such a corpse, that this martyr would rise?'[30] Julia Kristeva has argued that Dostoevsky's appeal to an ideal is an attempt to bear witness from an alternate space, free from the tyranny of trauma.[31] The appeal to an ideal excludes the crime or wound from time and stamps it with a symbolic configuration, an array of signs. This, for her, is tantamount to an offer of forgiveness. It turns the writer's lacerating affect into a healing effect addressed to readers. The wounds of the writer's flesh open the reader up for a gift of grace, perhaps like the Gothic windows and arches that proliferate in Dostoevsky's manuscripts in this period. But do they actually achieve anything more than a mere impression?

Exhausted by his exertions over *The Idiot*, increasingly frustrated by life abroad, Dostoevsky spent much of 1869 wallowing in lethargy. His sole achievement was *The Eternal Husband*, which, perhaps unjustly, he subsequently described as 'a most disgusting novella'.[32] He published it in *Zaria* (The Dawn), a new conservative journal to which he had long promised a full-fledged novel (as mentioned in the ditty above); this commitment continued to weigh on his conscience. In August the family moved from Florence to Dresden, where Anna gave birth to a daughter, Lyubov. The autumn was largely spent in frustrating negotiations for publishing contracts and loans. On multiple occasions he travelled to casinos in desperate attempts to try to earn money; invariably he lost every penny and needed Anna to wire him money for the frigid return journey (frigid, because he usually left his coat at a local pawnshop). He had been hoping for a lucrative edition of *The Idiot*, but gradually (and prematurely), in the face of critics' indifference, came to view the novel as a failure. He nurtured a grandiose idea, 'The Life of the Great Sinner', which over five separate novels would trace the life of a Russian intellectual from the 1840s to the 1870s, and which he would send to *Zaria*. The second novel, Dostoevsky insisted, would take place in a monastery, requiring extensive research in situ. Dostoevsky compared the scale of the conception to Tolstoy's *War and Peace*, which he had been reading with great interest as its instalments were published in *Russkii vestnik*. In the meantime Dostoevsky felt stranded abroad, unable to return to Russia for fear of being imprisoned for his unpaid debts. Amid the usual complaints about his health one encounters notes of desperation.

Most worrying was his artistic paralysis. Closely following events in Russia – 'I read *three* Russian newspapers to the final line and subscribe to two journals'[33] – Dostoevsky felt fully up to date on the 'idea' of Russian life, but he was in danger of losing touch with its 'flesh': 'and how this affects artistic work!'[34] To bide his time and earn much-needed income, Dostoevsky conceived a short novel for *Russkii vestnik* directed against radical ideological tendencies among the youth. The conception of the novel coincided with the sensational murder of a student who was accused of betrayal by the leader of a radical cell, Sergei Nechaev. Detailed reports of the conspiracy emerged only after the novel had commenced printing, giving Dostoevsky another occasion to boast with his Pauline bombast that he had 'prophesied facts'.[35] Dostoevsky could have learned of the events from other sources. As it happened, Anna Dostoevskaya's brother Ivan was a student at Moscow Agricultural Academy where the cell was based, and the leader of the group, Sergei Nechaev, had previously been championed by Mikhail Bakunin, the father of Russian anarchism, whose activities Dostoevsky had monitored while living in Geneva. Of course, Dostoevsky could also draw on his personal experiences of political conspiracy from the late 1840s; perhaps he saw the novel as a means of atonement. Amid all his personal connections to the subject, the novel on Nechaev was conceived 'less from the artistic than from the tendentious side': 'let it be even a pamphlet, but at least I'll speak my mind. I hope for success.'[36] It would only take him a few months.

In a letter of 9 October 1870 Dostoevsky summarized the political idea for Maikov:

facts have shown us that the illness that afflicted civilized Russians was much stronger than we ourselves imagined, and it was not

A page from a notebook for *The Idiot*, *c.* 1867, with sketches of characters and calligraphic exercises with the words 'Nero' and 'Ariman'.

limited to the Belinskys, Kraevskys, etc. But here occurred what the Evangelist Luke testifies to: the demons dwelt in the man, and their name was legion, and they begged Him: command us to enter into the swine, and He allowed them to. The demons entered into a herd of swine and the entire herd threw itself from a cliff into the sea and everything drowned. When the surrounding population gathered to see what had happened they saw the former demoniac dressed and seated at the feet of Jesus, and eyewitnesses told them how the demoniac had been healed. The exact same thing has happened with us. The demons have left Russian man and have entered into a herd of swine, that is, into the Nechaevs, Serno-Solovyeviches etc. They have drowned or will certainly drown, and the healed man whom the demons have left is seated at the feet of Jesus. Thus it was meant to be. Russia has puked forth the disgusting matter it was fed with, and nothing Russian is left in these puked-out rascals. And note, my dear friend: whoever loses his nation and nationality loses the faith of his fathers and God.[37]

In fact, though, Dostoevsky proved incapable of sacrificing his art to his ideas and embarked on yet another literary experiment that absorbed his creative energies and the attention of the Russian reading public until the end of 1872. The crucial change in the project occurred in the summer of 1870, after Dostoevsky suffered a series of debilitating epileptic attacks. He welcomed the new artistic plan, though he lamented the delay in publication (and in payment, and thus in his return to Russia). On 29 August 1870 he wrote to his relative Sophia Ivanova:

If only you knew how difficult it is to be a writer, that is, to bear this fate! Believe me, I know for certain that if I only had two or three years to work on this novel, like Turgenev, Goncharov or Tolstoy, I would write such a work that a hundred years later they would still be talking about it! [. . .] The idea is so good, so significant, that I myself bow down before it.[38]

One thing that happened to change Dostoevsky's plans was the sudden flood of anti-nihilist pamphlets appearing at the time in Russia. In October 1870 Nikolai Leskov's *At Daggers Drawn* began to appear in *Russkii vestnik*, Dostoevsky's home journal. However it is difficult to argue with Dostoevsky's assessment that Leskov's novel contains 'a lot of the devil knows what, as if the action is taking place on the moon'.[39] Leskov only strengthened Dostoevsky's belief that, in order to prove effective, the ideas of the novel had to find compelling artistic form. Having set out to 'fight texts with texts', Dostoevsky was brought back to his ideal of using text to create life.[40] The novel ended up satirizing the inanity of the '"promiscuous" production and circulation of printed matter'.[41] This led Dostoevsky to synthesize the political idea with the metaphysical ambitions of the 'Life of the Great Sinner'. Returning to the understated connections in *The Idiot* between modern psychology and nihilism, this would be a novel about the ways in which inward matters of conviction and character become expressed outwardly in conspiracy and catastrophe.

Failing as a spiritual testament, *The Idiot* also exposed problems of form which Dostoevsky had to resolve if his fiction was to instigate the desired ethical response. It was not just Dostoevsky's protagonists who had proved incapable of action; there was also the problem of the narrator. Myshkin, with his paralysed agency, is like the author of fiction, all-seeing and all-knowing, but a stranger to the world he regards, incapable of averting the catastrophe which his story requires as its ending. As Myshkin's stare gradually glazes over, Dostoevsky seems suddenly plagued by doubt about the efficacy of fiction as a form of moral action. In the final part of the novel Dostoevsky's narrator ties himself in knots over the limits of his knowledge and his ability to represent events in an adequate manner. The novel ends less in an apocalyptic explosion, than an implosion of the protagonists' consciousnesses.

Dostoevsky's solution to the inherent instability of literary meaning was to destabilize his narrative even more.[42] The fulsome narrator of *Demons*, Anton Lavrentievich G—v, is no less beset by insecurity than the nameless narrator of *The Idiot*, foisting himself on the reader's attention from the very first page, calling attention to his own 'lack of ability' and dwelling on the qualities of his knowledge. However, for crucial stretches of the novel, including extensive private conversations between characters where the narrator could not have had access to eyewitness information, we are given no information on the origin of his knowledge or the point of view. Fully cognisant of the limits of his knowledge, the narrator offers a total fiction that (in accordance with Dostoevsky's theories) could do justice to those aspects of reality which anyway remain unseen. Vladimir Alexandrov describes G—v as 'a cunningly wrought figure whose function is to manipulate the reader into becoming a co-conspirator in Dostoevskij's own artistic tactics'.[43]

Another consequence of G—v's patently inconsistent narration is that his informants' points of view constantly seep through, allowing all the characters a degree of control over the course of the story. As Michael Holquist has written, 'the typical relation of the novel's protagonists to each other [is] *essentially that of an author to the characters he invents*'.[44] This is particularly evident in two key relationships. Stepan Trofimovich Verkhovensky is, like Dostoevsky, a man of the 1840s, an author whose controversial works forced him into internal exile. Or so he believes, apparently as a way of excusing his utter failure actually to write. He is encouraged in this illusion by his patron Varvara Petrovna Stavrogina, who (the narrator says) 'invented him and was herself to believe in her invention. He was something like her dream'.[45] Harmless in himself, Stepan Trofimovich is shown to be culpable of a fatal abdication of ethical duty vis-à-vis the younger generation, whom he has given nothing save self-serving fictions.

The novel seems headed in a comic direction until the arrival of Nikolai Stavrogin, Varvara's son, whom Verkhovensky's son Pyotr Stepanovich idolizes as a revolutionary saviour. The younger Verkhovensky has gathered a revolutionary cell of dreamers and rascals who are awaiting the signal for action. When his idol baulks, however, Verkhovensky asserts his control: 'I invented you while I was abroad.'[46] Verkhovensky is transparently modelled on Nechaev, a cynical puppet-master surrounded by sycophantic idiots. But this does not explain where Stavrogin gets his power and what motivates him to go along with Verkhovensky's schemes. He could be an Iago (Dostoevsky's manuscripts show he was thinking about *Othello*), but Joseph Frank finds him more redolent of the Byronic demonism of Pechorin from Mikhail Lermontov's *Hero of Our Time* (1840) – and therefore profoundly anachronistic, a Romantic interloper in a hard-nosed, realist world.[47]

In *Demons* Dostoevsky confronts the limits of his poetics; he even has Stepan Trofimovich parody his own formulation of realism: 'My friend, real truth never seems plausible, do you know this? In order to make truth seem plausible, you must never fail to mix in a bit of lie.'[48] If the power of narrative rests largely in the power of the character or face which it describes, then the ruling criterion for judging among narratives becomes the charisma of character. Most of Dostoevsky's characters perform limited ideological roles that leave them two-dimensional, if fascinating caricatures. In creating a hero capable of bearing the burden of originality, Dostoevsky drew on his ideas about the 'Great Sinner' and on the original plan for *The Idiot*, in which the prince had been an artist of evil. Indeed, Stavrogin's name, based on the Greek word for 'cross' (*stauros*), testifies to the sacred charisma of his role. Unlike the other characters, who would reveal themselves in conversations reported by the chronicler, this central character could only reveal himself, as Dostoevsky explained in a letter to Mikhail Katkov: 'I will note one thing: I have sketched this entire character in scenes, in action, and not in ideas; therefore there is hope that it will emerge as a face.'[49] The rub was that, as Dostoevsky knew from previous experience, faces tend to have lives of their own. As René Girard noted in his study of *Demons*: 'The title of hero of a novel must be reserved for the character who triumphs over metaphysical desire in a tragic conclusion and thus becomes *capable of writing the novel*.'[50] Dostoevsky had to create a character capable of usurping his own power as author.

Dostoevsky's characterizations stand in complex relation to those of European realism. The Gogolian type, Dostoevsky asserts, 'is quite often only half of the truth, and half of the truth quite often is a lie'.[51] Dostoevsky's characters are undoubtedly types, but at the same time they are profoundly individual, eccentric, even improbable. This use of type was to a certain degree traditional in Russian literature. Yuri Lotman identified a similar use of type in Pushkin's *Eugene Onegin* and in the literary tradition it engendered, which sought to augment the sense of realism or veracity of characters by freeing them from the literary convention of harmony and completion. Next to the open-ended character, the author ended up on a par with the reader, and the world of the novel became seen as 'a fragment of living life'.[52] That is, in the Russian tradition the type was often less a representational category than a revelatory one. Nonetheless, Dostoevsky took the improbability of character to new extremes that he incurred the dismay of such contemporaries as Ivan Goncharov, who upbraided Dostoevsky in a famous letter of 1874. As Donald Fanger comments,

> For a realist like Goncharov, the mere fact that a character
> may *seem* improbable already constitutes an artistic fault:

A page from a notebook for *Demons*, *c.* 1871, showing Dostoevsky's calligraphic exercises with the words 'Venetian', 'Othello' and 'Desdemona'.

'You say yourself that "such a type is arising"; forgive me if I let myself note a contradiction here. If it is arising, then it is not yet a *type*.'[53]

In his own defence Dostoevsky appealed to his concept of realism, based less upon observation than upon intuition into 'the new guise of the universal that is just coming to birth'.[54] Dostoevsky's characters, Fanger observes, 'are compounded of contradictions, always in flux, always liable to realize in action some potentiality hitherto dormant'.[55]

Insensitive to his 'dormant' potentiality, however, Stavrogin serves as the conduit of destructive ideologies in which he does not believe and which virally supplant the personalities they infect. Each of the other characters becomes strangely dependent on Stavrogin, who is, however, totally unable or unwilling to perform the role he has assumed. There are two partial exceptions to this: Kirillov, the theomachist man-god, and Shatov, who idolizes the nation as the bearer of God without believing in God. (Though Shatov's views are close to Dostoevsky's, his name, derived from *shatkii*, identifies him as a 'wobbly' exponent of them.) Even they, however, appear as fragments off Stavrogin's massive homunculus, or else masks by which he conceals his own facelessness. Both Kirillov and Shatov are on the brink of establishing sincere inter-personal contact when they are destroyed in the wave of violence unleashed by Verkhovensky with Stavrogin's silent compliance. Shatov's and Kirillov's struggles with the divine follow the sado-masochistic logic of dominance and servitude that typified the modern psychology in Dostoevsky's eyes. Stavrogin is the kind of person who would be capable of a more transformative relation to the divine. Hannah Arendt noted how many of Stavrogin's actions appear unmotivated and gratuitous, that is, free of the forces of necessity, but short of actual freedom.[56] For Charles Olson, 'Shatov's blow upon Stavrogin's face is a more significant, whole and vital gesture than all the violent career of Stavrogin himself.'[57]

The novel ends with Stavrogin's suicide in the Swiss canton of Uri: 'On the table there lay a scrap of paper with the words written in pencil: "No one to blame. I myself."'[58] In death he seems a lot like Kirillov, his absolute egotism revealing a squalid and tongue-tied cynicism. It is worth considering what kind of a resolution would have been presented had Dostoevsky not been forced by his editor Katkov to omit a crucial chapter of *Demons*, which delayed completion of the novel for an entire year. In the chapter 'At Tikhon's', Stavrogin shows to a retired bishop a written confession of his rape of a young girl who, deciding that she has 'killed God', committed suicide while Stavrogin (in an echo of Ippolit's dream) watched a red spider climbing up a houseplant.[59] As J. M. Coetzee has shown, Stavrogin tries to avoid directly engaging the wily Tikhon in a verbal duel, keeping in reserve 'a certain kernel of identity he wishes to claim for himself'.[60] The only way to get beyond the casuistry of the ego would be to commit oneself to dialogue, the space of *logos*, in which (as with Raskolnikov and Sonya) one would open oneself to the active concern of the other and, potentially, of grace. As with *Notes from Underground* in 1863, however, Dostoevsky found himself blocked from elaborating a direct link between the sordid tale and its spiritual solution. Despite the trouble he had reconceiving the ending to compensate for the loss of 'At Tikhon's', he refrained from restoring the omitted chapter when publishing *Demons* as a book.

Both *The Idiot* and *Demons* end with the hero's demise in Switzerland, a negative space of bourgeois neutrality, where at the very time Dostoevsky was writing the young Friedrich Nietzsche was confronting some of the same insights: the death of God as a psychological reality for modern man, the concomitant breach in ethical values, and the need for a new model of individuality. When he discovered Dostoevsky in the late 1880s, Nietzsche certainly recognized the similarities in their diagnoses of modernity, though he could not have shared Dostoevsky's favoured plans of treatment, linked as they were to the political role of Russia and the religious role of Eastern Orthodoxy. The comparison of Dostoevsky and Nietzsche became de rigueur for Russian philosophers and European Modernists such as D. H. Lawrence. What is often forgotten in these comparisons, however, is that for Dostoevsky the modern condition is not only a historical event, but also a result of actions for which individuals ultimately remain responsible. Stavrogin is neither a result nor a symptom of the 'death of God'; he is a perpetrator. The demons represent the very forces of resistances within history and narrative, those darknesses within time that shade direct sources of light, creating the 'slanting rays' that illuminate Dostoevsky's novels. Dostoevsky does not compel readers to accept any of his conclusions; however, one can reject the metaphysical horizon of Dostoevsky's novels only by slamming them shut.

When Adelaida Epanchina asks Prince Myshkin for the subject of a painting, he immediately thinks of 'the face of a man condemned to death a minute before the guillotine's blow'.[61] 'What face? Just a face?' asks Adelaida in shock. 'What a strange subject, and what kind of picture would it be?' The prince elaborates: 'A cross and a head – this is the picture: the face of the priest, of the executioner, and of his two helpers, and also several heads and eyes below. All of this can be drawn in the background, in the mist, as an accessory . . . That's the kind of picture.'[62] Both Myshkin and Stavrogin end up as just such detached heads set off by crosses suspended nearby like guillotines. One thinks of the portraits that float across Dostoevsky's manuscripts. Must the portrayal of a hero always end as a beheading?

As early as August 1838, not yet seventeen years old, Dostoevsky had written to his brother Mikhail: 'I have a project: to go mad. [. . .] It is frightful to see a man in possession of the unknowable, who does not know what to do, who plays with a toy that is God!'[63] This play is manifested most directly in the characters which possessed Dostoevsky and by which he continues to possess our world. Dostoevsky discovered that the shape of narrative would not lead his characters to redemption, only to apocalypse. Moreover, he discovered that, as in *Crime and Punishment*, his desire to create a face capable of bearing the grace of redemption could also lead to a mask liable of being possessed by demons and of usurping his own power as creator. One wonders at the obsessive consistency with which Dostoevsky continued to probe the same problems, tell the same stories and peer into the same faces. The 'new story' he sought could only occur in the world outside of the fiction. The need to endow these faces with living flesh led him back to Russia, back into the course of life. The human figures Dostoevsky sketched in the manuscripts of his next novel, *The Adolescent*, became fuller figures, but they continued to abide under the imminent threat of erasure.

7

Gestures of Engagement

On 21 March 1874 Dostoevsky found himself back in jail. His offence was, this time as in 1849, political in nature, but infinitely less grave in degree. On an official visit to Emperor Alexander II in Petersburg, Sultan-Mahomet Sultan-Kyrgyz had begun his speech in confident style, but when the emperor interrupted him to ask, 'So you speak Russian?', the sultan lost his nerve and could not continue. By printing notice of this occurrence in the weekly newspaper *Grazhdanin* (Citizen), which he had been editing since the end of 1872, Dostoevsky violated the censorship restrictions on reporting the personal actions or words of the emperor and members of the court. He was fined 25 roubles and ordered to spend 48 hours in the detention cells of the very same police station on Haymarket Square in St Petersburg where Raskolnikov had confessed his crimes. The duty officer took the opportunity to discuss *Crime and Punishment* with its famous author.

Ironically the newspaper was one of the most loyal to the imperial cause, having been founded in 1872 by the ultra-conservative Prince Vladimir Meshchersky (1839–1914), who was known as 'Prince Full-stop' for his hostility towards reform. Though as a former political convict he remained under surveillance by the police until 1875, for many years Dostoevsky had been describing himself as a passionate supporter of the Emperor, who soon after his accession in 1855 had liberated the serfs and seen through many other reforms, but who had subsequently alienated much of enlightened society by failing to deliver on a constitution. In a letter to Apollon Maikov, written from his temporary exile in Geneva at the beginning of April 1868, Dostoevsky wrote:

> our constitution is the mutual love of the monarch for the people and of the people for the monarch [. . .] Here abroad I have become a complete monarchist for Russia. If anyone has done anything in Russia then it, of course, is he alone (and not just for this, but simply because he is a Tsar beloved by the Russian people, and personally because he is Tsar. In Russia the people has given and continues to give any Tsar its love and believes only in him. For the people this is a sacrament, blessing, and anointing.)[1]

The anti-radical thrust of *Demons* had confirmed Dostoevsky as a leading voice in conservative circles. As the author of *Notes from Underground*, *Crime and Punishment* and other troubling works, however, Dostoevsky was a notoriously unreliable ally.

Dostoevsky's editorship of *Grazhdanin* was a surprise success, raising the number of subscribers threefold to 3,000. He initially viewed the job as 'rest from artistic work' but before long was complaining of its demands, writing to historian Mikhail Pogodin on 26 February 1873:

> the images of stories and novels swarm in my head and form in my heart. I conceive them and note them down, every day adding new features to the written plan, and at the same time I see that all of my time is taken up by the magazine, that I can no longer write, and I fall into regret and despair.[2]

He had weathered previous run-ins with the censors over articles about the famine of 1873, but his ridiculous detention was the final straw; Dostoevsky resigned the editorship, ostensibly for health

Vasily Perov, *Fyodor Dostoevsky*, 1872, oil on canvas.

reasons, and set about writing a new novel, which would become *The Adolescent*. Dostoevsky remained closely associated with *Grazhdanin* in following years, aiding his beleaguered Viktor Putsykovich as the newspaper lost circulation, was forced to close in early 1879, and was briefly resurrected as *Russkii Grazhdanin* in Berlin, where Putsykovich travelled to escape his debtors. As late as 1878 Dostoevsky contributed to *Grazhdanin* a humorous story of a Triton found in a city pond, which he signed with the name of Kuzma Prutkov, a popular but wholly fictional comic poet.

Dostoevsky's tutelage of the *Grazhdanin* is most notable for the *Writer's Diary* which he published on its pages. Dostoevsky conceived the *Writer's Diary* as 'a report about all my actually experienced impressions as a Russian writer, a report about everything seen, heard and read'.[3] Prompted by Dickens's *Master Humphrey's Clock* (1840–41), Dostoevsky had been nurturing the idea since at least 1866. In *Demons*, which he was still completing when he accepted the editorship of *Grazhdanin*, one of the characters suggests publishing a kind of almanac 'in which everything can find a place':

> Of course, anything could be included: curiosities, fires, donations, all sorts of good and bad deeds, all sorts of pronouncements and speeches, perhaps even news about flooded rivers, perhaps even some government decrees as well, but with the choice only of those things that might portray the epoch; everything would be included with a certain view, a direction, an intention, an idea, throwing light on the entire whole, the totality. And, finally, the book should be interesting even as light reading, to say nothing of its being an indispensable reference work! It would be, so to speak, a picture of the spiritual, moral, inner life of Russia over an entire year.[4]

The *Writer's Diary* took up some of the burden of Dostoevsky's earlier experiments with 'notes', which captured nascent social tendencies. It was also an attempt to transform the relationship between the writer and his audience into a more interactive exchange. As such, the *Writer's Diary* served as a laboratory of sorts for Dostoevsky's fiction, a space in which he set about reinventing the writing practices that had just begun to bring him such success. The stories that appeared in the *Writer's Diary* (three over the fifteen issues for 1873) are particularly interesting, occupying a kind of intermediary status between documentary and fiction. After focusing on *The Adolescent* for the better part of two years, Dostoevsky returned to the *Writer's Diary* as his main occupation in 1876 and 1877.

During his four years abroad (April 1867 to July 1871), Dostoevsky had come to feel alienated from 'the living stream of life; not from its idea, but from its flesh – and how this affects artistic work!'[5] For the next five years (1873–7) Dostoevsky immersed himself in this muddy stream, studying current social phenomena like 'the social environment' and 'the accidental family'. He now satisfied his hunger for theatre and other spectacles at the courts, where he attended numerous scandalous trials of the decade. Even after returning to Russia Dostoevsky remained an itinerant, frequently changing apartments in less savoury areas of Petersburg, as he had throughout his life. To make it worse, having been entrusted with his stepfather's possessions, Pavel Isaev had sold off all his books, rendering Dostoevsky's existence uncomfortably bare. Though he was renowned for his profligate ways, through the *Writer's Diary* (and with his wife's business savvy) he would reinvent himself as a successful literary entrepreneur, turning his readers into a community of regular subscribers.

The tone for the *Writer's Diary* was set early on by the essay 'Environment' (published in *Grazhdanin* on 8 January 1873), in which Dostoevsky takes on those who excuse crime with theories of social determinism. After playing out the argument with a querulous imaginary opponent, Dostoevsky concludes that by denying the criminal's freedom to do otherwise we are simply trying to excuse our own failures. On the contrary, holding him responsible affirms our own moral freedom to change our physical environment: 'Energy, labour and struggle: this is how the environment becomes reworked. Only labour and struggle can achieve sovereignty and a sense of one's own dignity.'[6] In support of his argument Dostoevsky refers to his own experiences among criminals: 'it may be that not a single one of them avoided long emotional suffering within himself, a suffering that is the most purifying and invigorating'.[7]

Frequently these semi-ideological, semi-intimate essays lead into anecdotes that veer towards entire fictional stories. The first example of this is 'Vlas' (published in *Grazhdanin* on 22 January 1873), which begins with a quotation from Nikolai Nekrasov's 1855 poem of the same title about a criminal who has become a spiritual wanderer. Dostoevsky says that he recently heard a similar story handed down by a monastic elder about a man who crawled to him begging forgiveness for a blasphemous deed. On a dare he stole communion bread during liturgy and took aim at it with a gun: 'It remained only to shoot, but suddenly before me there stood a cross, and on it the Crucified One. Here I lost consciousness and fell with my rifle.'[8] Dostoevsky begins by considering what this says about the power of Russians' conscience, even among 'village nihilists',[9] which holds blasphemy as the worst sin and understands that only suffering can atone for it; it is sensitive to 'mystical terror'.[10] But as he examines the act further he replays the story as a psychological study, comparing it to one of a man condemned to death:

And lo, at the very final moment, the entire lie, the entire baseness of the act, all the cowardice which he had taken for strength, all the shame of the fall, all of this escaped suddenly, in a single instant, from his heart and stood before him in an awesome form. An incredible vision appeared to him . . . everything ended.[11]

But why, Dostoevsky asks, did it appear as an image, 'a completely external fact, independent from his spirit'?[12] Indeed, was the vision real or a mere hallucination? Dostoevsky seems to elide the very difference. Whether this new resurrection is real or imaginary, fact or fiction, it has a real effect on Vlas. Dostoevsky appears to affirm that Christ will rise triumphant from out of this new death at the hands of the nihilists. This faith is short-lived, however: true to the spirit of the *Writer's Diary*, in the very next issue Dostoevsky published the story 'Bobok', in which a washed-out, drunken writer overhears a conversation amongst the residents of a cemetery, who continue their petty and lascivious posturing even in the grave. Nihilism proves most insidious when it is at its most banal.

The relationship between documentary and fictional modes in Dostoevsky's writing in the 1870s is illumined by the essay 'At the Exhibition', published on 26 March. Here Dostoevsky reiterates his longstanding rejection of tendentiousness in art, lamenting that because of the call for social relevance 'a young poet resists his natural need to pour forth in his own images [. . .] and forces himself painfully to produce a topic that satisfies the general, uniform, liberal and social opinion'.[13] Addressing the tradition typified by the radical critics Nikolai Chernyshevsky and Nikolai Dobrolyubov, Dostoevsky continues: '"One must represent reality as it is", they say; meanwhile there is no such reality and there never has been on earth, because the essence of things is inaccessible to man and he perceives nature as it is reflected in his idea and filtered through his feelings.'[14] This aesthetic leaves painters in the dominant genre tradition with the impossible task of capturing the idea and the as yet unrealized potential within 'contemporary, flowing reality', which is of necessity disfigured, unsightly and inchoate.[15] The best they can do, like Ilya Repin in his *Barge Haulers on the Volga* (1873), is to try to avoid imposing stereotypes on their figures: 'Now that's almost a picture', Dostoevsky exclaims.[16]

Dostoevsky's solution is, in his terms, to 'mix' genre painting with historical painting, which allows one to view 'flowing reality' from the distance of its idea. The historical painter must capture

Vasily Perov, *Hunters at a Campsite*, 1871, oil on canvas.

both the original moment and the future potentiality that will make this moment worthy of commemoration. He finds no good examples of this in contemporary painting, merely singling out Nikolai Ge's *The Last Supper* (1863) for its failure to live up to this standard, judging it 'entirely incommensurate and disproportionate to the future'.[17] It would be better to give Christ a face, as in Titian's *The Tribute Money* (1516), which he knew from Dresden: 'then a lot would immediately become clear'. As it is, however, 'Mr Ge chased after realism' and ended up with 'falsity and a preconceived notion'.[18] This, in a nutshell, remains the central problem of Dostoevsky's aesthetics: to provide an image of fluid reality that would be 'commensurate and proportionate' to an as yet unknown future. Thus Dostoevsky set about reinventing the novel yet again in response to this task.

Breaking the pattern he had set with *Crime and Punishment*, Dostoevsky published *The Adolescent* not in the conservative *Russkii vestnik*, but in *Otechestvennye zapiski*, a journal now edited by his old rival Nikolai Nekrasov and associated with progressive – even radical – opinion. Indeed, *The Adolescent* is an odd work, even by Dostoevsky's standards, panned by critics and ignored by subsequent generations of readers. It broke Dostoevsky's string of metaphysical thrillers – *Crime and Punishment* (1867), *The Idiot* (1870), *Demons* (1873) – to relate the story of an 'accidental' family in the words of its illegitimate and ambitious scion. As a story *The Adolescent* never really gets going, oscillating between the narrator's fixation on the people around him and his obsessive self-analysis. It contains Dostoevsky's most egregious lapse of concentration, when after a prolonged absence the character Darya Onisimovna re-emerges in Part III as Nastasya Yegorovna. One critic complained: 'the author has got too bogged down in a mass of details that are extremely petty and uninteresting for anyone save himself; meanwhile the main story of the novel doesn't move forward at all'.[19] The novel is known mainly for several speeches which appear to develop Dostoevsky's views on politics and art in interesting directions, though the character who gives the speeches – the vain nobleman Versilov – is a far from trustworthy source. It might well be dismissed as a stillborn project if not for the fact that it falls between two such masterpieces as *Demons* and *The Brothers*

Ilya Repin, *Barge Haulers on the Volga*, 1873, oil on canvas.

Titian, *The Tribute Money*, *c*. 1516, today in the Staatliche Kunstsammlungen, Dresden.

Karamazov. Normally a harsh critic of his own books, Dostoevsky refused to concede that it was a lesser work.

The Adolescent can be redeemed as a risky experiment in fictional form which, through the stumbling first-person narration, enacts the difficulty of deriving and maintaining an imaginary grasp on reality at a time of rapid social and cultural change. In particular, the plot involves a constant contention of images, from the icon and Claude Lorrain's mythic landscapes to photography. This contention of images is not only an incisive analysis of modern media in Russian society; it also constitutes a study of the aesthetics and ethics of representation itself. *The Adolescent* shows Dostoevsky deconstructing the modern novel as a means of investigating the breakdown of the modern family, about which he had learned so much while at work on the newspaper *Grazhdanin* and the *Writer's Diary*. It is a first-person narrative by Arkady Makarovich Dolgoruky, the illegitimate son of the nobleman Versilov and the wife (Sophia) of one of Versilov's servants, Makar Dolgoruky. Raised in a foster home, Arkady dreams of acceptance by Versilov, whom he calls 'my future father'.[20] At the same time, he is consumed by the 'idea' of getting rich through '*diligence* and *constancy*' or, in his shorthand, of 'becoming a Rothschild'.[21] Caught between the shame and the pride of being a self-made upstart, his unstable identity is captured by his surname: though it belongs to a pious servant who agreed to conceal Versilov's parentage and his own wife's infidelity, it evokes associations with one of the grandest old Russian lineages (Prince Yuri Dolgoruky was the purported founder of Moscow in the twelfth century). When introducing himself Arkady is commonly asked '*prince* Dolgoruky?', to which he is obliged to answer, 'no, just plain Dolgoruky'.[22] Always on the defensive, he finds himself trying to claim his illegitimacy as a virtue. However, like the Underground Man, he finds himself constantly being defined from outside and unable to assert himself as a sovereign individual.

Thus Arkady undertakes to shape his own story, but here again he finds himself constrained by convention. He rejects the model of literary autobiography because of its implicit egotism, rhetorical structure and mercantilism: 'I am not a *littérateur*, I don't want to be a *littérateur*, and would regard it improper and base to drag the inside of my soul and a beautiful description of my feelings onto the literary market.'[23] Instead Arkady addresses his 'notes' to a 'fantastic' reader of the future.[24] The notes read at times like an uncorrected first draft: 'I've just re-read what I wrote and see that I am much more intelligent than what I wrote. How does it end up that what an intelligent man says is much stupider than what he keeps to himself?'[25] Yet write he must: 'I write as a man who has long since become sober and in many ways as a bystander; but how can I depict my sadness at that time (which I now vividly recall) [?]'[26] Prevented from availing himself of normal conventions of representation, Arkady faces the task of creating new literary resources commensurate to the remarkable personality he wants to be.

One of Arkady's main strategies is to focus on visual representations, especially the human faces he encounters, which both imprint experience and are themselves imprinted on the memory. Meeting Versilov for the first time in nine years, for instance, Arkady notes that 'life had imprinted on this face something much more curious than before'.[27] Arkady claims to have marked his mother's face so clearly that he recognized her years later when he met her accidentally.[28] But the imprint is not indelible; Makar tells Arkady that 'The limit of man's memory is set at only a hundred years', since after a hundred years there pass from the earth 'all who have seen his living image'.[29] Moroever, Arkady is not so sanguine about the power of his own face to express his personhood. His own mirror-image tells him his face is 'ordinary'.[30] Versilov suggests that Arkady's problem might be that his 'idea' is too frankly visible on his 'honest face', which implies (as in *Demons)* that ideas can never really be a stable basis for human personhood.[31] Similarly Arkady concludes that Versilov is a 'fantastic doll', 'just my dream, a dream of childhood years. It was I myself who invented him that way, but in fact he turned out to be otherwise and fell so far below my fantasy'.[32] The face is a field where the imprint of historical life and the projection of fantasy contend for primacy.

The distinction between imprinted and projected images would seem to be especially salient in the discussions of technologies of visual representation, which imprint faces in potentially more powerful and lasting ways. The first detailed study of images in the novel occurs in Arkady's description of Versilov's apartment, which still shows 'the remnants of the comfort it once had':

> in the living room, for instance, there was a quite decent porcelain lamp, and on the wall there hung an excellent engraving of the Dresden Madonna and, directly opposite, on the other wall, an expensive photograph, of enormous size, of the cast bronze gates of a Florentine cathedral. In the corner of the same room there hung a grand case with ancient family images, of which one (of All Saints) had a large gilded silver casing [*riza*], the very one that they had meant to pawn, while the other (an image of the Mother of God) had a velvet casing, embroidered in pearl. Before the images there hung an oil-lamp that was lit for each feast. Versilov was evidently indifferent to the images in the sense of their meaning, only wrinkling his nose sometimes, restraining himself it seemed, from the lamp light that was reflected off the gilded casing, complaining meekly that it harmed his vision; but he still refrained from preventing mother from lighting the lamp.[33]

Each image here is heavily mediated, essentially transposed from an original medium into a secondary one: engraving from a painting, a photograph from metal work, and icons covered with protective metal casings. These transpositions blur the border between technologies of imprinting (engraving, photography) and those of projection (painting, illumination). Moreover, the images are shown to depend on their illumination. But even this fails to secure their effect. Surrounded by images, Versilov remains free not to see. His indifference betrays a reluctance not only to see or even to acknowledge the very illumination that enables vision.

The icon is a particularly sensitive kind of image. Late in the novel Arkady tells the story of a compromising letter of which he had gained possession and which might threaten Versilov's impending marriage to Katerina Nikolaevna. Arkady finds himself obliged to 'jump ahead', anticipating the course of events, and the reader becomes lost in a complex web of temporal markers, in which Arkady, like a clumsy Proust, anticipates the future only to remark on his retrospective interpretations of events that have not yet occurred or been narrated. One morning Arkady awakes refreshed after a dreamless night and sets off for the funeral of his foster father, Makar Dolgoruky. At the wake Arkady remarks upon the presence of Makar's old icon:

> One detail I marked only too well: Mama was sitting on the sofa, and to the left of the sofa, on a special round side table, there lay an image that was as if especially prepared for some-thing; it was an ancient icon, without a metal casing, only with [metal] crowns above the heads of the saints, of whom two were depicted. This image belonged to Makar Ivanovich; I knew this and I also knew that the dead man never parted with this icon and regarded it as wonder-working.[34]

The icon has been willed to Versilov, who turns up at the wake and gives Sophia a bouquet of flowers, shocking the mourners, especially when he admits that on his way there he had been tempted three times to throw the bouquet onto the snow and crush it with his boot. 'You know, I feel like I am bifurcating and am horribly afraid of this', Versilov declares as he notes the icon: 'What is this image? Oh, the dead man's, I remember. It was his familial icon, his grand-father's; he never parted with it; I know, I remember, he willed it to me; I really recall . . . and, it seems, it's a schismatic [*raskol'nichii*] image . . . let me take a look.'[35] Spinning the icon in his hands, he threatens to smash it on the corner of the stove: 'I am certain that it will immediately break [*raskoletsia*] into two halves, no more and no less.'[36] Beginning himself to bifurcate, Versilov snatches the icon and snaps it into two against the corner of the stove. The splitting of the icon figures allegorically the schism within the Russian Church and the splitting of Russian society that had been at the heart of the character Raskolnikov, who also ended up at a crossroads in order to 'put an end to something'. Makar probably belonged to the schismatics, and Versilov's iconoclasm allies both men with the forces of disintegration, countered here (as in *Crime and Punishment*) by female wisdom (Sonya = Sophia). There is an inevitability to the loss of the icon, and, as so often in Dostoevsky's works from *Crime and Punishment* to 'The Gentle Creature', the icon is impotent to counteract it. Yet Versilov's blindness to the images that surround him makes him all the more susceptible to their power. As Arkady tries to discover the story behind Versilov's actions, he overhears a conversation between Versilov and his fiancée: 'I knew I was eavesdropping, eavesdropping on somebody else's secret, but I remained. How could I not remain? After all, there was the double. After all, he had already destroyed the image in my eyes.'[37] By destroying Makar's family image, Versilov destroys Arkady's image of him, which undermines Arkady's ability to act ethically.

The moral quality of organizing the manifold into a discrete image is called throughout *blagoobrazie*, literally well-imagedness, a virtue most explicitly linked with the righteous Makar Dolgoruky. Makar is also sensitive to images (icons, most notably) and an accomplished storyteller. Arkady relates one of Makar's stories, about a village tyrant who causes the death of his rival's widow's children, most spitefully that of the eldest son, who drowns in a river as he flees the man's wrath. The man is reformed, first commissioning an oil painting of the fatal scene, then marrying the widow with the promise that he will build a church in the boy's memory, and finally departing to wander as an itinerant monk. The painting is a crucial stage in the man's moral reformation, but it attains its power only with the completion of the conversion, when the man attains a life of humility and asceticism. Images might provide the surest ethical guides, but their correct reading also requires spiritual detachment.

Against the icon and devotional painting stands the photograph; Dostoevsky registers an ambivalence about the photograph as a mechanical technology that, at the same time, might provide the most direct imprint of reality. The first instance concerns a photograph of Sophia hanging in Versilov's study which stuns Arkady with its 'spiritual likeness' to the original, 'as if this was a real portrait by an artist's hand, and not a mechanical imprint'.[38] Versilov argues that this is an exceptional case for photography insofar as

the original, that is, each of us, is most rarely alike himself. Only in rare instants does the human face express its main feature, its most characteristic thought. The artist studies the face and intuits the face's main thought, although at the moment he is copying it it might not have been in the face at all. Photography, by contrast, finds man as he is, and it's quite possible that Napoleon might at one moment or another turn out dim-witted and Bismarck tender. Here, in this portrait, as if on purpose the sun caught Sonya at her dominant instant – of bashful, gentle love and somewhat uncouth, frightened chastity. Yes, she was happy at the moment that she finally became convinced that I thirsted to possess her portrait![39]

Arkady allows that a photograph might imprint potential that is invisible to the human eye and human intention. The same is implied when Arkady reflects on the image of an abandoned infant Arina, who had been entrusted to his care:

> The girl's tongue, lips and mouth were covered with a fine white powder, and towards evening she died, staring at me with her big black eyes as if she already understood. I don't understand why it didn't occur to me to take a photograph of her, the little dead thing.[40]

Earlier in the novel Makar suggested that memory and image are not projected from the individual outwards, but are rather gifts from those who surround one. Arkady seems to recognize the responsibility that has been thrust upon him for retaining of the infant's imprint. The infant becomes linked to Makar in Arkady's memory; both instantiate the aesthetic and ethical harmony of which Arkady dreams:

> I lay face to the wall and suddenly in the corner saw the bright, radiant spot of the setting sun, the very spot that I awaited yesterday with such curses, and I remember that it was as if my soul leaped up and as if a new light penetrated into my heart. I remember this sweet minute and care not to forget it. This was merely an instant of new hope and new strength . . . I was recovering, and therefore these impulses could be an inevitable consequence of the state of my nerves; but even now I believe in that very radiant hope – that's what I wanted to note and remember. Of course at that moment I knew for sure that I would not go wandering with Makar Ivanovich and that I knew not myself what comprised this new aspiration that filled me, but one word I had already pronounced, albeit in delirium: 'They have no well-imagedness [*blagoobrazie*]!' 'Of course', I thought in a frenzy, 'from this minute forth I shall seek "well-imagedness," and they lack it, and therefore I shall leave them.'[41]

Seeing Versilov and his minions seated next to Makar, Arkady complains that 'for me to see you all next to this infant (I pointed to Makar) is an unsightly disgrace [*bezobrazie*]'.[42] Arkady then dreams of his various enemies surrounding him and ridiculing him for his ideal of well-imagedness; they remove their masks to reveal a diabolical chaos of distorted 'features'. Arkady interprets the dream as revealing his own 'spider's soul'.[43]

Failing as a *Bildungsroman*, the novel finds itself obliged to reconstitute the very possibility of image (*Bild*, *obraz*), no longer as a static object, but as a dynamic force within consciousness and history. *The Adolescent* is a story – albeit a halting one – of the emergence of the possibility of a new literary image. Reflecting on his narration, Arkady again returns to the story of the icon:

> I am horribly sad that in the course of these notes I have fre-quently allowed myself treat this man [Versilov] disrespectfully and condescendingly. But as I wrote I was too much imagining myself precisely as I was in each of the minutes I described. Finishing my notes and completing the final line, I suddenly felt that I have re-educated myself, precisely by the very process of memory and notation.[44]

Arkady's language here suggests the model exemplified by St Augustine's *Confessions*: reading his own story as it imprinted itself on the page, the author is able to gather together the mani-fold of time into an image of an eternal present, highlighting the design of the whole and illumining each discrete moment with its purposefulness vis-à-vis the whole. Thus, Arkady suggests, narra-tive produces presence only obliquely, so to speak, between the lines.

This thirst for a new image is confirmed by Arkady's former guardian Nikolai Semyonovich, to whom Arkady sends his manu-script for review. In his response Nikolai Semyonovich notes that the destructive desires (or *bezobrazie*) of Arkady's characters might reveal a subconscious thirst for 'order and "well-imagedness"'.[45] In short, Nikolai Semyonovich suggests, it might be the role of literature to provide the consummate form that society lacks:

> Oh, in the historical genre one can depict a multitude of pleasant and joyous details! One can so enthral the reader that he will accept an historical picture as one possible also in the present. Such a work, if executed with great talent, would belong less to Russian literature than to Russian history. This would be an artistically complete picture of a Russian mirage, but one that really existed until people realized that it was a mirage.[46]

Nikolai Semyonovich admits that such a task is beyond Arkady, the scion of an 'accidental family' and the 'novelist of a hero from an accidental family': 'This is a thankless task and one without beautiful forms. After all, these types, at the very least, are a fluid matter and therefore cannot be artistically completed.'[47] At the most, such 'notes' could 'serve as material for a future work of art, a future picture, which would be disordered but still survive the epochs'.[48] 'At least some true features will survive so that one might guess from them what could lurk in the soul of an average adolescent of that troubled time, knowledge that would not be completely worthless since generations arise from adolescents.'[49] Arkady's tale is thus offered to the reader as 'notes towards a novel' – the novel of a much different future society.

In March 1875 Dostoevsky responded to criticism of his novel by drafting a new preface:

> I am proud that I was the first to capture the real man *of the Russian majority* and was the first to expose his monstrous and tragic side. This tragism consists in the consciousness of monstrosity [. . .] Only I have captured the tragism of the

underground, consisting in suffering, self-punishment, in the consciousness of something better and the impossibility of reaching it, and, most importantly, in the clear conviction of these unfortunates that, since everyone is like this, there is no point in self-improvement. What can support those who try to improve? A reward, faith? There's no one to give a reward, no one to believe in! One more step and one gets extreme perversity, crime (murder). A mystery.[50]

While Dostoevsky might have aspired to the Augustinian ideal of the eternally present image, he regarded this ideal as impossible in his own awkwardly adolescent time. This was an age that could not sustain the icon and would have to rediscover the image in media more attuned to its own unsightly chaos.

For all of its fascinating dialogue, *The Adolescent* failed to provide Dostoevsky with the kind of formal breakthrough he sought in his novels. At the end of 1875 he announced that he was resuming his *Writer's Diary*, which evidently remained the best place for Dostoevsky not only to exercise his thoughts about art, society and politics, but also to work out new artistic forms capable of transfiguring these thoughts into effective forces. His approach is exemplified by the autobiographical essay 'The Peasant Marei' in the January issue of the *Writer's Diary*, in which he remembers a moment in the camps when, surrounded by drunken convicts singing 'unsightly, disgusting songs' and fighting among themselves, he recollects a moment from his childhood: an August day when, at the age of nine, he wandered around his family's village, gathering twigs to beat frogs with, when he heard someone yell, 'A wolf is coming!' In fright he ran up to the peasant Marei, who comforted him 'with some maternal and broad smile'.[51] The memory allows the convict Dostoevsky (now aged 29) to view the simple men who surround him in the prison camp 'with a different gaze' and also, sixteen years later still, to draw on this transfiguration to support his faith in the power of Russian religious and folk traditions: 'we must bow down before the people [*narod*] and await from it everything, both thought and image.'[52] More important than this *profession de foi*, however, is the mechanism of this transformation of memory into image and then into text: 'It began from some points, some mark, sometimes unremarkable, and then gradually grew into a complete picture, into some strong and complete impression.'[53] It is this 'triple vision', as Robert Louis Jackson terms it, that unites memory and impression into its 'crucial artistic embodiment'.[54]

In his *Writer's Diary* Dostoevsky usually combined distinct registers of discourse in a complex weave that resists being sorted into tidy categories like 'fiction' and 'commentary' or even 'essay'. Still, one is drawn especially to those instances where Dostoevsky's commentary on current events is suddenly hijacked by fictional set pieces (for which, strangely enough, Dostoevsky invariably apologized to his subscribers). In October 1876 Dostoevsky included a section entitled 'Two Suicides', which begins with the declaration that life is always more profound than art:

Not long ago I happened to be speaking to one of our writers (a great artist) about the comical aspects of life and the difficulty of defining a thing and giving it its proper name [. . .] 'But do you know', the writer said to me suddenly, apparently deeply struck by his long-held idea, 'do you know, whatever you write or portray, whatever you set down in a work of art, you can never match real life. It doesn't matter what you depict – it will always come out weaker than real life. You might think you've found the most comical aspect of some certain thing in life and captured its most grotesque aspect – but not at all! Real life will at once present you with something of this same sort that you never even suspected and that goes far beyond anything your own observation and imagination were able to create! . . .'

[. . .] In truth, if you investigate some fact of real life – even one that at first glance is not so vivid – you'll find in it, if you have the capacity and the vision, a depth that you won't find even in Shakespeare [. . .] But of course we can never exhaust a whole phenomenon and never reach its end, or its beginning. We know only the daily flow of the things we see, and this only on the surface; but the ends and the beginnings are things that, for human beings, still lie in the realm of the fantastic.[55]

This train of thought led Dostoevsky to pen one of his most remarkable stories, 'The Gentle Creature: A Fantastic Story', which he apologetically offered to his readers in lieu of a regular issue of the *Writer's Diary* for November 1876. Dostoevsky proceeds by requesting the reader's indulgence for the form of the work, 'not a story and not notes', which relies on the assumption of a 'stenographer' who might record the protagonist's speech, just like in Hugo's *The Last Day of a Man Condemned to Death*. Why, one might ask, is Dostoevsky suddenly stumbling over such an unavoidable and even banal precondition of fiction: the author's assumption of impossible knowledge, especially about other people's emotions and thoughts? By foregrounding the conceit Dostoevsky implicates the reader in the construction of this impossible, but real supplement to 'fact'.

With this notion of 'stenography' the brief preface also underscores the link between the story and Dostoevsky's own writing practice. The story begins with the suicide of the unnamed wife of the protagonist, a pawnbroker. Pacing the room where her corpse lies, he tells their twisted story and explains why it was that, despite his love, he arrived a mere 'several minutes too late' to prevent her suicide. They had met when, a poor orphan, she had brought her icons to his pawnshop. After marriage their relationship became increasingly adversarial, to the point that they ceased speaking. Once he awoke to find her pointing a gun at his head. After she throws herself from the window in despair, clutching her icon in a final attempt to redeem her soul from his clutches, the protagonist finds himself so wracked with grief that he regards himself, not her, as victim, that is, as the loser of the duel: 'No, I'm serious: when they carry her away tomorrow, what will I do?'[56] One can't help seeing here a reflection of Dostoevsky's relationship with his own much younger wife, to whom he dictated many of his later works. It shows how conscious he was of the ways in which the stenographic recording of his 'fantastic' visions inscribed her – and by extension his readers – into the economy of violence and domination he so deplored.

In the spring of 1876 Dostoevsky got talking to Ivan Goncharov on the street in St Petersburg. Goncharov, who had previously been so critical of Dostoevsky's atypical protagonists, confessed to feeling jaded by the world he had spent his life investigating in such detail: 'I cherish my ideals and everything I have loved in life [. . .] and I want to spend the few years left to me with this; it is burdensome for me to study these creatures (he gestured towards the crowd passing by on Nevsky Prospekt).'[57] This 'study', Dostoevsky added, was the precise purpose of *Writer's Diary*. It was an exercise in banishing – or at least managing – disgust with 'facts' by chronicling their fantastic development in the imagination. Soon after announcing a hiatus from his *Writer's Diary*, on 28 February 1878, Dostoevsky wrote to one correspondent with çone of his standard complaints about liberals who 'love humanity terribly', but only 'in general': 'If humanity is made incarnate as *a man*, as *a face*, then they can't even bear this face or stand next to it because of disgust for it.'[58] The very same day he wrote to another correspondent about his own fear of being such an invidious presence:

You think I'm one of those people who save hearts, resolve souls and dispel grief? Many write such things to me, but I know *for sure* that I am more capable of inciting disappointment and disgust. I am not good at lulling people to sleep, although I have sometimes tried.[59]

8

Pilgrimage

On 23 June 1878, accompanied by the young philosopher Vladimir
Solovyov (1853–1900), Dostoevsky embarked on a brief pilgrimage
to the monastery Optina Pustyn', in the province of Kaluga, which
turned out to be much more distant and isolated than these two
confirmed urbanites anticipated. It was a return of sorts to the
lost world of his childhood, but Dostoevsky was beside himself
with grief. On 16 May – a month earlier – he and his young wife
Anna had lost their three-year-old son Aleksei to a sudden onset
of epilepsy, which the boy had evidently inherited from his father
but which had not previously been diagnosed. Aleksei was the
second of their children to die, after Sophia in 1868; two others,
Lyubov and Fyodor, born in 1869 and 1871 respectively, survived
into adulthood. Dostoevsky and Solovyov stayed at Optina for
three days, 25–7 June, during which time Dostoevsky met
repeatedly with the elder Amvrosii (or Ambrose, 1812–1891).
Throughout the journey Dostoevsky discussed with Solovyov
his plans for a new novel, *The Brothers Karamazov*, which was
to take place in part in a monastery. Many of the details of monastery life in the novel reflect Dostoevsky's experience over these
three days, for instance the depiction of grieving mothers and the
advice given them by the elder Zosima. Moreover, its young hero
was given the name of the Dostoevskys' deceased son Aleksei. In
the most immediate sense, the novel is a therapeutic hymn to the
memory of a child.

Unknown photographer, *Vladimir Solovyov, c.* 1877.

Dostoevsky had never really been an avid traveller, perhaps because his first long journey had been to a prison where he spent four years as a political prisoner, followed by six years in exile. His journeys to Western Europe in the early 1860s were dictated largely by his need to escape the constraints of home and engage in experimentation – not only in his art, but also in gambling and in erotic adventure. His longest period of wandering – when he was forced to escape his debts in 1867, immediately after marrying Anna – had been one long purgatory. After returning to Russia in July 1871, he left the country again only in June 1874 to take the waters at Bad Ems, stopping off in Geneva to visit the grave of his daughter Sophia. His epilepsy now compounded by emphysema, Dostoevsky returned to Bad Ems three times, where he continued work on his projects – *The Adolescent* in 1874–5, the *Writer's Diary* in 1876 and *The Brothers Karamazov* in 1879. He claimed to be 'frightfully sensitive' to the waters, but whatever physical benefit he derived was tempered by the irritations of travel, cheap hostels with noisy neighbours, and his limited German (this despite his claim, first recorded in 1861 and repeated in 1880, that 'any Russian can speak all languages and study the spirit of each foreign language to fine detail, like his own Russian language').[1]

While at Ems he took particular pleasure describing to Anna (who remained home in Russia) the unappealing aristocrats and nouveaux riches that surrounded him, writing on 21 July 1876:

> I bought a printed sheet of visitors: a multitude of Russians, but all either *Stroganoff* or *Golitzin* or *Kobyline, chambellan de la cour,* and even then only wives and families, not [the men] themselves; or else Russian Jews and Germans, of the banking and brokerage trades. Not a single acquaintance.[2]

Family tied him ever closer to home. In 1875 he professed to Anna: 'I've become frightfully womanish [*obabilsia*] at home these last eight years. I can't part from you even for the shortest time; that's what it's come to.'[3] By 1879 it was worse: 'Anya, it's unbearably hard and unpleasant for me here, almost no easier and no [less] unpleasant than the prison camp I experienced. I say this *without exaggeration*', he wrote, underlining the final words for good measure.[4]

Still, despite its disruptions and claustrophobia, travel to the fantasy-land of Western Europe continued to arouse Dostoevsky's literary imagination and erotic desire. Apart from a brief flirtation with Pelageya Guseva at Bad Ems in the summer of 1875,

Dostoevsky seems mostly to have kept his erotic energy for his letters to Anna: 'I dream seductive dreams of you', he wrote in 1874. 'There's no one better *in this sense* than my Anechka. Don't be a prude when you read this.'[5] His letters to Anna bear witness to the close proximity between the sacred and the profane in his imagination. Completing the section of *The Brothers Karamazov* on Zosima, whom he calls 'Pater Seraphicus', in 1879 Dostoevsky wrote to Anna of his desire for his 'mistress and sovereign':

> I have become convinced, Anya, that I not only love you, but I am in love with you and you are my one and only sovereign, and this after twelve years! I mean this in the most *earthly* sense, despite the fact that you have changed and aged since I first saw you at the age of nineteen. But now, do you believe, I am attracted to you in that sense *incomparably more* than then. This might seem improbable, but it is so. True, you are still only 32, and this is the age of a woman's flowering [. . .] If you were a bit more open with me you would be perfection itself. I kiss you every minute in my dreams, *all over, every minute* passionately. I especially love that about which it has been said: 'And he is ravaged and intoxicated by this thing.' – This thing I kiss every minute in every way, and I fully intend to keep kissing it all my life.[6]

Anna did turn out to be a bit of a prude, crossing out portions of this and other letters to safeguard the morals of posterity. Still, it is clear that, even at the moment of Dostoevsky's most spiritual creation, he remained a committed sensualist.

Certainly Dostoevsky had never conceived of his own art separately from his embodied existence. Since marrying Anna in 1867, Dostoevsky had become deeply dependent upon her for his material welfare. Displaying an enviable entrepreneurial streak, she organized the subscription to the *Writer's Diary* in

1876–7 and published separate editions of Dostoevsky's more popular works: *Demons*, *Notes from the Dead House*, *Crime and Punishment*, even *The Idiot* and *The Adolescent*, which had originally seemed such flops. The income helped the Dostoevskys to stabilize their living situation in St Petersburg; after all their forced peregrintions, the Dostoevskys stayed at one apartment on Grecheskii Prospekt for almost three years (from September 1875 to May 1878), before settling in their final abode in Kuznechnyi Lane in October 1878, where they stayed until Dostoevsky's death. In 1876 they also purchased a small house in Staraya Russa, a small resort town near ancient Novgorod, several hours south of Petersburg by train, where they had been holidaying since 1872. Giving Dostoevsky his first detailed experience of the Russian provinces since his return from exile, Staraya Russa would serve as a model for the Karamazovs' town of Skotoprigonyevsk and as a refuge for work on his final novel. It was from Staraya Russa that, in June 1878, Dostoevsky travelled to Optina Pustyn'. It was only after he established a home that he could undertake a pilgrimage.

Throughout the 1870s – and up to the very day of his death – Dostoevsky was engaged in a withering legal tangle over the estate of his wealthy aunt Aleksandra Kumanina, who died in 1871. Although he had redeemed his claim with a one-time payout of 10,000 roubles in 1864, after the death of his brother Mikhail, he now sued to be restored as an heir, ostensibly on behalf of his sisters, who as women did not stand to inherit at all. His motives were constantly questioned, however, both by the other (unrelated) heirs and by his own sisters. At times he suggested that he was driven primarily by his concern for his own children's financial security. Anna Dostoevskaya felt that he was less interested in the money than in the prospect of owning land, especially a woodland. This yearning for land reveals the extent of the trauma he experienced from the loss of his birthright.

Postcard of a fire tower, Staraya Russa, late 19th century

In July 1877, while staying with the family of Anna's brother in Malyi Prikol, Dostoevsky paid a visit to his family's estate, Darovoe (then owned by his sister Vera Ivanova), for the first time since his youth, reporting in the *Writer's Diary*: 'this small and unremarkable place made the deepest and strongest impression on my for my entire subsequent life, where everything is full of the dearest memories for me'.[7] His use of some local place names in *The Brothers Karamazov* has suggested to some readers that Dostoevsky folded memories of his childhood into the novel, perhaps even depicting his own father as the despicable Fyodor Pavlovich. Since so little is known about his father and the circumstances of his death, this is sheer speculation. However the trip to Darovoe did provoke one of Dostoevsky's most extended essays on fatherhood, published as part of the *Writer's Diary*:

The need and worry of their fathers are reflected from childhood in [children's] hearts as gloomy pictures, as reminiscences of sometimes the most poisonous kind. Into their deep old age children remember their fathers' pusillanimity, family squabbles, arguments, accusations, bitter rebukes and even curses [. . .] and, worst of all, sometimes remember their fathers' baseness, their shameful actions out of ambition or money, disgusting intrigues and sickening slavishness. [. . .] Only an equally great faith is capable of engendering *beauty* in the memories of children [. . .] There are even cases where a father who has fallen lowest, but who still retains in his soul at least a distant former image of a great thought and great faith in it, has been able to transplant into the receptive and thirsting souls of his pitiful children this seed of a great thought and a great feeling, and was then forgiven sincerely by his children for this single act of benevolence, despite all the rest.[8]

Dostoevsky's impassioned plea to fathers reads both as a pledge before his own children and as an expression of his broader concern for the young generation of Russians in the 1870s, rooted in his regret for having been a poor son to his country. Since his impris-

Dostoevsky's house in Staraya Russa today.

onment, with growing alarm he had chronicled the rise of at least two new generations of 'Russian boys', each of which seemed intent on compounding the mistakes of their fathers. Proust remarked that Dostoevsky's oeuvre might be summarized as 'the story of a murder', but it might just as well be called 'fathers and sons', a title that occurs in his notes for *The Brothers Karamazov*.

The interweaving of material considerations with the spiritual and the artistic is evident in a letter Dostoevsky wrote to Anna from Bad Ems on 13 August 1879:

> My dear, I think constantly of my death (I think about it seriously here) and what I will leave you and the children with. Everyone thinks we have money, but we have nothing. Now I am burdened with the *Karamazovs*; I need to finish it well, to craft it like a jeweller, but it is a difficult and risky thing and will claim much of my strength. But it is also a fateful thing: it should establish my name; otherwise there is no hope. I will finish the novel and at the end of next year will announce a subscription for the [*Writer's*] *Diary* and with the subscription money will buy an estate.[9]

Dostoevsky hoped that *The Brothers Karamazov* would bring him full circle, not only restoring the social status and hereditary capital he had long ago sacrificed to his vocation, but confirming the curative influence of the images he gave to the young. With all this in mind, he decided to dedicate the novel to Anna. The death of his son in May 1878 imperilled these hopes and set Dostoevsky on a new cycle of despair. Perhaps it was natural that he sought to address this despair by returning even more decisively to his childhood faith.

Dostoevsky's turn to the institutions of the Orthodox Christian Church confirmed his identification with the so-called Slavophile tradition in Russian thought, which had received its authoritative statements in the work of Aleksei Khomiakov (1804–60) and Ivan Kireevsky (1806–1856). Kireevsky in particular had spent time in Optina Pustyn' and had corresponded with the elder Makarii (or Macarius), one of Amvrosii's illustrious predecessors. Under the influence of the German Idealists, especially Friedrich Schelling (1775–1854), the Slavophiles had argued for the insufficiency of abstract reason alone and the need for broader concepts of wisdom, which Kireevsky called 'integral knowledge' or 'knowledge of the heart'.[10] United in such knowledge, which is open to myth as well as to science, communities would preserve the character of a spiritual congregation, what the Slavophiles called *sobornost'*. As the movement progressed, it also became increasingly nationalistic and sometimes militant, as in the writings of Dostoevsky's nemesis Konstantin Leontyev (1831–1891). Such ideas resonate in our day not only through rampant nationalism in Eastern Europe, but also in the sometimes violently anti-modern and anti-Western extremes of religious fundamentalism all over the world. The more radical forms of these ideas were frequently linked to monastic centres like Optina Pustyn', where Leontyev spent several years before taking monastic vows in 1891.

From the mid-1850s Dostoevsky consistently claimed allegiance to traditional Orthodoxy as a resource for national renewal and a gift that Russia bore for the world. In 1870 he wrote to Apollon Maikov:

> Russia's entire destiny is Orthodoxy, the *light from the East*, which will flow to the blind humanity of the West which has lost Christ. The entire misfortune of Europe – everything, without any exception – occurred because they lost Christ with the Roman Church, and then decided they could get by without Christ.[11]

In the late 1870s he became a friend of the conservative statesman Konstantin Pobedonostsev, a mentor of sorts to the future Alexander III. Dostoevsky frequently boasted of his detailed knowledge of Russian monasticism, gained during family visits in childhood. Upon arriving back in European Russia in 1859, after four years in a penal colony and six more in distant exile, he had revisited the St Sergius-Trinity Monastery outside Moscow. At difficult moments he often spoke of going as a pilgrim to Mount Athos and Jerusalem, the holiest sites in the Orthodox Christian world. The characters of Tikhon in *Demons* and Makar in *The Adolescent* result from Dostoevsky's stated attempt to create what he called 'a majestic, *positive*, holy figure' and to inject the spirit of Orthodox wisdom and humility into secular stories of contemporary society.[12] In particular both *The Adolescent* and *The Brothers Karamazov* testify to Dostoevsky's careful reading of *The Tale of the Pilgrimage and Travel of Athonite Monk Parthenius in Russia, Moldavia, Turkey and the Holy Land* (1856), a contemporary classic of spiritual literature which Dostoevsky took abroad with him in 1867.[13] His brief journey to Optina Pustyn' was 'a long-standing dream', according to his wife Anna.[14] It is notable, though, that both of his recorded pilgrimages were linked to the death of his children; they could be seen as inspired more by an emotional need, than by a religious one.

Dostoevsky's Christianity was profoundly idiosyncratic. Writing to his brother in 1840, Dostoevsky compared Homer to Christ as 'a fabled man [. . .] made incarnate by God and sent to us'.[15] When in prison in 1849 he pointedly asked his brother to bring him the New Testament in French translation, indicating that he was more interested in its literary than its devotional qualities. His favourite religious paintings were all Western and post-medieval. In 1870, sketching out the character of the future Stavrogin, he became fascinated with Konstantin Golubov, a disciple of the sectarian Pavel of Prussia (1821–1895); though he expounded a traditional pietistic moralism, Golubov had corresponded with the radical political theorist Nikolai Ogaryov and represented a model of a forward-looking, engaged Christian intellectual.

Dostoevsky's study of Russian religious culture in *The Brothers Karamazov* immediately became probably the most influential representation of Orthodoxy to the world (even to Russians themselves). At the time, however, it was attacked by critics like Konstantin Leontyev, who saw its 'humanitarian' spirit as issuing from Western sources:

> Mr Dostoevsky is apparently one of very few thinkers who has failed to lose faith in *man himself*. [. . .] Democratic and liberal progress believes more in the forced, gradual correction of humanity, than in the moral force of the person [. . .] Christianity believes absolutely neither in the one nor in the other, i.e., neither in the better autonomous morality of the person, nor in the reason of collective humanity, which will sooner or later create heaven on earth.[16]

Leontyev contrasted Dostoevsky's 'rosy' Christianity to the ascetic discipline actually practiced at centres like Optina Pustyn' by monks who tended to look much more like the stern disciplinarian Fr Ferapont than his rival Fr Zosima. This, for example, is a brief story from Parthenius' *Tale* about Elder Leonid of Optina Pustyn':

> Among these people there knelt a gentleman who had come to the monastery for worship and to visit the great elder. The elder asked him: 'And what do you desire to receive from me?' The gentleman answered in tears: 'I desire, o holy father, to receive from you an edifying instruction'. The elder asked: 'Have you fulfilled what I previously ordered you to do?' He answered: 'No, holy father, I can't fulfil it.' The elder said: 'Why have you come to request something else when you haven't fulfilled the

first thing?' Then he angrily told his disciples: 'Kick him out of my cell.' And they kicked him out.[17]

How different is Dostoevsky's vision of the St Francis-like Zosima, chatting with the birds and other small creatures, patiently accepting all manner of humiliation.

This desire for a modern Orthodoxy explains Dostoevsky's interest in Vladimir Solovyov, who presented a more sophisticated and respectable version of Slavophilism in the 1870s. In 1878 Dostoevsky attended Solovyov's *Lectures on Divine Godmanhood*, where social critique was embedded in a grandiose cosmological scheme *à la* Friedrich Schelling's *Ages of the World*. Solovyov's doctoral dissertation, *The Critique of Abstract Principles* (1877–80), was published serially in *Russkii vestnik* alongside Dostoevsky's *Brothers Karamazov*. Its orientation towards 'integral knowledge' was a powerful development of Slavophile notions:

By abstract principles I mean those individual ideas (the particular aspects and elements of a universal idea) which,

Resurrection Cathedral in Staraya Russa.

when abstracted from the whole and confirmed in their exclusivity, lose their true character and, entering into opposition and conflict with one another, plunge the world of man into that state of intellectual disorder in which it has hitherto found itself.[18]

Solovyov extends his critique of rationalism into a critique of socialism, ending up with a vision of society that he calls 'free theocracy', that is, rule by the church.

The moral significance of society [. . .] is determined by the religious or mystical principle in man, by virtue of which all members of a society do not form limits to one another but inwardly complete one another in a free unity of spiritual love, which must find immediate realization in a spiritual society or church. Thus the foundation of a normal society must be a spiritual union or church that itself defines the indisputable aims of society.[19]

Dostoevsky was indubitably impressed and inspired by his young friend's arguments. However, Dostoevsky also lent Solovyov's arguments to his character Ivan, the one who silently acquiesces to his illegitimate brother Smerdyakov's murder of their father and then descends into delirium. In art if not in life, Dostoevsky found any doctrinal solutions, even the most sympathetic, to be dangerous oversimplifications capable of constraining humans' ability to act freely and in accordance with the conditions of material life.

It is worth noting how curious Dostoevsky was about the occult. Not so very long before their visit to Optina Pustyn', Dostoevsky joined Vladimir Solovyov on a visit to an English soothsayer named Mrs Field. Though he attacked spiritism repeatedly in the *Writer's Diary* for 1876, a curious note from 1878 shows him eagerly following debates about a provincial quack's attempts to access the fourth dimension by means of knots made in a length of string.[20] All of these currents are evident in Dostoevsky's fascination (shared by Solovyov and Leo Tolstoy) with the apocalyptic ravings of Nikolai Fyodorov (1827–1903), a visionary librarian whose belief in the metaphysical unity of humanity led to a pseudo-scientific project for the resurrection of all who have ever lived, 'the resurrection of our fathers', as Fyodorov termed it. Writing to Fyodorov's disciple, Dostoevsky declared that 'we here, that is Solovyov and I, believe in real, literal and personal resurrection, and that it will occur on earth.'[21]

Throughout his life Dostoevsky's wholehearted engagement with modernity had put his Christian faith under intense pressure. Though Orthodox Christianity often appealed to Dostoevsky's love of paradox, he could not accept the church's categorical interpretations of such puzzles as the first Beatitude: 'Blessed are the poor in spirit, for theirs is the kingdom of heaven' (Matthew 5:3). In the novel *The Idiot* Nastasya Filippovna's benefactor (and, it is rumoured, her seducer) Afanasy Totsky notes her apparent shyness and remarks that 'just such ones love to wield power'.[22] The cruel children of *The Brothers Karamazov* also give some hints of what might happen if the meek were really to inherit the earth. For Dostoevsky, subjugation and power were implicated in a complex, violent dialectic, which cannot be healed by wishful thinking, but must be actively reshaped.

Moreover, as Susan McReynolds has demonstrated, Dostoevsky had always been profoundly troubled by the logic of sacrifice that lies at the core of Christian belief and, by glorifying victimhood, threatens to cancel out Christian claims for social justice.[23] From the very beginning of his literary career Dostoevsky displayed a fascination with images of dead children.

However these images are no less impotent than the icons in the pawnbroker's house which look out helplessly upon the murders

The house in Staraya Russa that was supposedly the model for Grushenka's home in *The Brothers Karamazov.*

in *Crime and Punishment,* and the icon to which Raskolnikov's mother prays without result. They are no less haunting than Holbein's *Dead Christ,* testifying to the unresurrected body. *The Brothers Karamazov* is often read as a redemption of these images, especially when, at the end of the novel, Alyosha gathers the children around him in the name of the dead boy Ilyusha. As always, however, Dostoevsky gives some of the best lines to the sceptics, like Ivan Karamazov, who declares that he would return his ticket to God's heaven if admission is to be bought for the price of the single tear of a child.

Dostoevsky's sincere and longstanding interest in Christian monasticism was one strand in a complex weave of interests and commitments, the contradictions among which he resolved in his fiction. If the monastery Optina Pustyn' presented some kind of solution for the problems of modernity in Dostoevsky's understanding, it must still be shown how this played out in his literary imagination.

Though Anna did not accompany her husband to the monastery Optina pustyn', she did record for us what Dostoevsky told her about his trip:

> Fyodor Mikhailovich met with the then-famous 'elder' Fr Amvrosii three times: once in a crowd in front of many people and twice one-on-one, and he took away from their conversations a profound and penetrating impression. When Fyodor Mikhailovich told the 'elder' about the misfortune that had befallen us and about my excessively violent grieving, the elder asked whether I was a believer. When Fyodor Mikhailovich answered in the affirmative, he asked to convey to me his blessing and also the words which the elder Zosima later said in the novel to the grieving mother [. . .] From Fyodor Mikhailovich's stories one could see how profoundly this widely respected 'elder' knew and saw into the human heart.[24]

Anna writes the word 'elder' [*starets*] in quotation marks, for it was a relatively new concept in Russian Orthodoxy. It was part of a monastic revival inspired in part by the *Philokalia*, a collection of ascetic writings from the entire history of Eastern Christianity, from the desert fathers of the third century to St Gregory Palamas of the fourteenth. The *Philokalia* had been translated into Slavonic in the late eighteenth century by Paisy Velichkovsky, who lived in what is now Moldova. A Russian translation had appeared in 1877, making it more accessible to the lay reader. Aware of its relatively brief history, in his novel Dostoevsky provides a detailed definition of the *starets*: 'The elder is one who takes your soul, your will into his own soul and his own will. By selecting an elder, you detach yourself from your own will and give it to him in complete obedience, with complete self-detachment.'[25] Dostoevsky's choice of words suggests a deeper grounding in the Eastern Christian ascetic tradition. In *The Ladder* of St John Climacus (seventh century AD), detachment – *aprospatheia* – is the second step on the ladder of divine ascent:

> If someone has hated the world, he has run away from its misery; but if he has an attachment to visible things, then he is not yet cleansed of grief [. . .] No one can enter crowned into the heavenly bridal chamber without first making the three renunciations. He has to turn away from worldly concerns, from men, from family; he must cut selfishness away; and thirdly, he must rebuff the vanity that follows obedience.[26]

Dostoevsky saw the elder as a figure capable of reinvigorating the Orthodox Church, about which he noted in his final year: 'The church is in a kind of paralysis, and has been for a long time.'[27] Indeed, his novel did more than anything to legitimize the new institution of the elder and, in the process, begin a major change in the way Orthodox Christianity was understood in Russia and throughout the world. Sometimes overlooked in all this, however, is the role it played in the poetics in the novel.

Dostoevsky's interest in the elder reflects his consistent attraction to charismatic individuals, something that was not particularly common in Orthodox monasticism prior to the nineteenth century. This is reflected in the 'symbol of faith' which Dostoevsky expounded in a letter to his benefactor Nadezhda Fonvizina upon his release from the penal colony in 1854, where he had written that, 'if someone succeeded in proving to me that Christ was outside the truth, and if, *indeed*, the truth was outside Christ, I would sooner remain with Christ than with the truth.'[28] Dostoevsky's faith was never just a meek escape from the forces of harsh necessity, but a contrarian challenge against them, rooted in his faith in human potential – or at least the potential of certain remarkable individuals. This is both its power and its limitation. How can one avoid thinking of Stavrogin, who has similarly been invested with the wills of a group of would-be revolutionaries, but who ends up like the Gadarene swine, an empty vessel of demonic energy?

His statements of 1854 underscore the radicalism of Dostoevsky's definition of the monastic elder, who takes the place of Christ as the holder of the individual's will. Curiously, although Dostoevsky frequently attached his belief to charismatic seers, the image of the lonely spiritual wanderer is among the most comic in Dostoevsky's fiction. In *Crime and Punishment* the sinister Svidrigailov declares he is off to America before shooting himself in the head. Prince Myshkin is ridiculed as Pushkin's 'Poor Knight', a Don Quixote-type figure who bears Nastasya Filippovna's initials on his shield, while General Ivolgin, his latest story having been exposed as a pathetic lie, tells his young son to grab a travel bag and set off with him. The characters of *Demons* make pilgrimage to a holy fool, Semyon Yakovlevich, who turns out to be a malicious fraud. At the end of *Demons* Stepan Trofimovich sets off as a Russian Quixote, but he makes it only to the next village where he becomes ill and falls in love with a woman peddling gospels.

The Brothers Karamazov is more about brotherhood in the world than in the monastery, which is the site both of soaring spiritual ascents and the most reprehensible scandals perpetrated by Fyodor Pavlovich, the disgraceful and cynical patriarch of the Karamazov family. Following the narrative logic of his mature novels, Dostoevsky was intent on examining existing types (even that of the wise monastic elder) for human potentials beyond what is presently manifest or even possible. On 21 July 1878 Dostoevsky wrote to L. Grigoryev:

In my sympathies I do not at all belong to the sixties or even the forties. I like the present time more for there is something clearly coming to be, instead of what previously was [merely] prospective and ideal [. . .] in a word there has been attained and developed a *higher* idea. And, after all, if only there were higher ideas, or the beginning of higher ideas, then everything else would appear; it can all be consumed and corrected for the better.[29]

This is a political no less than a spiritual quest.

But, as I have insisted throughout this biography, Dostoevsky was an artist before all else. Dostoevsky's desire for compelling images often undermined the ideological point he was interested in communicating, even to the point that his repeated attempts 'to represent a positively beautiful man'[30] had led him into a repetitive cycle of rewriting the same story with the same outcome: the effective beheading of his heroes, who by becoming images cease to be flesh-and-blood people. Thus Dostoevsky's commitment to Orthodoxy – or rather Orthodoxy's influence on him – can be measured only by examining the degree to which the engagement with Orthodoxy helped to shape a 'positively beautiful man' – not just as a paragon of beauty, but as a real force in the modern material world, a world peopled less by Zosimas and Alyoshas than by Fyodor Pavloviches.

While in his fictions Dostoevsky wagered on artistic form to sort out the contradictions of his world, in his political writings he sometimes appears to resort to easy answers, most conspicuously by blaming the Jews. Susan McReynolds shows persuasively that Dostoevsky's discomfort with the logic of sacrifice was an important factor in his theological anti-Semitism, which made the Jews 'the repository of what he found objectionable about his Christian faith', namely the Job-like acceptance of suffering and sacrifice.[31] This theological anti-Semitism should be distinguished from the knee-jerk anti-Semitism that punctuates Dostoevsky's personal correspondence, and also from the unappealing portraits of Jewish characters in Dostoevsky's fiction from *Notes from the Dead House* to *Demons*. Distasteful as it is, his theological anti-Semitism appears to have been the product of intent thought and sincere belief, and therefore it requires our attention.

Dostoevsky's most extended treatment of the 'Jewish question' comes in the March 1877 issue of the *Writer's Diary*. Rejecting accusations of anti-Semitic prejudice, Dostoevsky insists that by pointing out the tensions between Jews and ethnic Russians he is not assigning blame, simply registering 'the character of the age'.[32] Nevertheless, he proceeds to blame 'the Jew' for these tensions, apparently regarding the Jews as the primary bearers of the spirit of exploitation that defines 'the character of the age' (which, incidentally, he calls 'Yidism'):

> I sometimes have a fantasy: what if there weren't three million Jews in Russia but three million Russians, and at the same time eighty million Jews. Well, what would the Russians turn into and how would they be treated? Would they be allowed equal

Viacheslav Klykov, *Monument to Dostoevsky*, Staraya Russa, 2001.

rights? Would they be allowed to pray freely? Wouldn't they be turned into slaves? Even worse: wouldn't their skin be flayed off? Wouldn't they be pounded into the dust, to the point of total extermination, as [the Jews] acted with foreign nations in ancient times, in their ancient history? No sir, I assure you that the Russian nation has no prejudicial hatred for the Jew, but it might not sympathize with him, especially in some places, even to a great degree.[33]

Asking how Russians can act in a Christian way towards Jews and other alleged exploiters without becoming their victims, Dostoevsky transfers the problem from the realm of newspaper reports and political discussions into that of fictional narrative, for it is here that the iron logic of exchange and retribution can be bent; it might even be broken for once and for all. He tells the story of an 'isolated case' which he has learned about from a female Jewish acquaintance. She has sent a report on the funeral of a Protestant German doctor who had worked tirelessly as a conciliator in a border town that has known racial tensions between the Jewish and Russian populations. The long quotation from the lady's letter concludes:

A pastor and a Jewish rabbi spoke at his graveside, and both wept; but he just lay there in his old, worn uniform coat with an handkerchief tied around his head – that dear head; and it seemed that he was sleeping, so fresh was the colour of his face . . .[34]

This case launches Dostoevsky into an excited tirade about this 'isolated' event as a work of art:

If I were a painter I would definitely paint this 'genre' scene [. . .] I'm awfully fond of realism in art, but some of our contemporary realists have *no moral centre* in their paintings, as one mighty poet and refined artist expressed it the other day [. . .] Here, in this subject I propose for a 'genre', there would be such a centre, I think. And it's a lavish subject for an artist. In the first place, there's the absolute, incredible stinking misery of a poor Jewish hut. One could even show a lot of humour here, and it would be awfully apropos: humour, after all, is the wit of deep feeling [. . .] Even the lighting could be made interesting: a guttering tallow candle is burning out on a crooked table, while through the single, tiny window, covered with ice and hoarfrost, there glimmers the light of a new day, a new day of toil for the poor people [. . .] The poor, newborn little Jewish baby is squirming on the bed before him; the Christian takes the little Jew in his arms and wraps him with the shirt taken from his own back. The solution to the Jewish question, gentlemen! [. . .] Will this come to pass? Most likely it will not, yet it could come to pass; and on earth one can do nothing finer than believe that this *can* and *will* come to pass.[35]

'Let it be! Let it be!' Dostoevsky exclaims, launching into the exalted prophetic mode that spills over into *The Brothers Karamazov*, where this phrase becomes the title of a central chapter.[36]

The next month Dostoevsky became wholly absorbed in the fight of the Bulgarians for independence from the Ottoman Empire, which had led Russia into war with Turkey. Dostoevsky sees the conflict as an inevitable consequence of the conflict of civilizations described by his colleague, the former Petrashevsky follower Nikolai Danilevsky, and by other pan-Slav theorists: 'the entire [Russian] nation has risen for truth, for the holy cause.'[37] He paints the fight as a ritual cleansing, part of Russia's own renewal as a Christian nation: 'Not always is war a scourge; sometimes it is also salvation.'[38] In particular, war only reveals the violence hidden by 'the long bourgeois peace', which proves unsustainable 'because of some pitiful stock-market interests, new markets necessary for exploiters, the acquisition of new slaves needed by the possessors of bags of gold, in a word, for reasons that cannot be justified by the need for self-preservation, but testify to the fickle and sickly state of the national organism'.[39] But if the body of the Russian state sacrifices itself in this way, won't it end up – like Christ's body in Holbein's painting, or like Zosima's in *The Brothers Karamazov* – a hollow, impotent failure of spirit?

Dostoevsky's troubling thoughts on the 'Jewish question' and the war with Turkey lead directly into a fictional story, 'The Dream of a Ridiculous Man: A Fantastic Story', which he offers as part two of the *Writer's Diary* for April 1877 and as a resolution of the conflicts he has been describing. The narrator, reminiscent of the Underground Man, professes to have become so 'indifferent' to life that he can't even get up the energy to shoot himself. Sitting with his gun, he begins thinking of a young girl who had asked him for help; unable to banish her from his thoughts, he finds himself questioning – and therefore contradicting – his indifference. Falling asleep, he dreams of travelling through space to another planet, a double of Earth, only before the Fall into sin. He admires their happiness, but finds himself missing the human emotions he had experienced on earth. Infected by his desire, the aliens experience a fall and become divided by falsehood, conflict and other hallmarks of human existence:

> When they became evil they began to speak of fraternity and humanitarianism and understood these ideas. When they became criminal they invented justice and prescribed for themselves entire codices in order to preserve it, while for the defence of the codices they established a guillotine. They only slightly remembered what they had lost and did not even want to believe that they had once been innocent and happy. They even laughed at the possibility of their previous happiness and

called it a dream. They couldn't even imagine it in forms and images, but, strangely and miraculously: having lost any faith in their former happiness, calling it a fairy tale, they so desired to become innocent and happy again that they fell before the desire of their heart, like children, deified this desire, built temples and began to pray to their own idea, their own 'desire', while at the same time believing in its impossibility and unrealizability, but deifying it with their tears and worshipping it.[40]

Awaking back on earth, the narrator feels animated by the 'living image' of his dream and goes off in search of the girl he had failed to help. As has happened numerous times before in Dostoevsky's fiction, the instant before death has expanded out and restored the possibility of the redemptive image, which in turn stimulates action in the world.

What fiction provides, then, is the possibility of sacrifice without a victim. It falls to the writer both to be sacrificial victim and to tell the tale of the sacrifice, to become 'ridiculous' by accepting fantasy as fact: in a word, to become a prophet. Dostoevsky felt uniquely qualified to be a writer in this vein since he knew what it meant to die and be revived. Conversely, one of Dostoevsky's most biting critiques of his nemesis Turgenev was that, at the execution of Jean-Baptiste Troppmann in Paris in 1870, he had averted his eyes at the last moment and then had the nerve to write about it:

Man, while he's on the earth's surface, has no right to turn away and ignore what is occurring on the earth; for this there are supreme *ethical* reasons. *Homo sum et nihil humanum . . .* etc. Most comical of all is that he turns away at the last minute and doesn't see the execution: 'Look, gentlemen, how sensitively I have been brought up! I couldn't bear it'. But he gives himself away: as a result the main impression of the article is a frightful concern for himself, to the final degree of squeamishness, for his self-preservation and his peace of mind, and all this in sight of a head that's been chopped off![41]

For Dostoevsky, the points at which grace settles in the world are always tears in the world's material fabric: wounds, gifts and suspended instants. Dostoevsky's task, in the final analysis, was to make his affective fiction into the communication of such stigmata.

At the time of Dostoevsky's interventions, Orthodoxy was a far from settled quantity, more a potentiality which, like so many aspects of modern Russian culture, hung in the balance. Dostoevsky's intervention was decisive because it shifted the definition of Orthodoxy from the realms of doctrine and custom to that of aesthetics, eventually contributing to a rediscovery and reevaluation of the icon and other artefacts. At the same time, Dostoevsky empowered aesthetics for the first time to make a decisive difference in the self-understanding of Orthodoxy. As poets and artists began to see their dedication to form as a discipline, so ascetic practice became inseparable from the search for beauty. In his youth Dostoevsky had imagined 'no ascetic holier than the poet'.[42] Following the narrative logic of Dostoevsky's mature novels, Orthodox thinkers would increasingly seek grounds for redemption in the very shape of a world that seemed to exclude it as a possibility.

It is therefore an over-simplification merely to identify Dostoevsky's position on Christianity with the figure of Zosima. Undoubtedly Dostoevsky saw himself reflected partially in Zosima's hopeful self-abnegation and willingness to seem ridiculous to the world. However, he remained conscious of the difference between Zosima's ascetic practice and his own aesthetic work. Writing to his editor Nikolai Lyubimov, Dostoevsky explained:

It stands to reason that many of the sermons of my elder Zosima (or, rather, their means of expression) belong to his

7A page from a notebook relating to *The Brothers Karamazov*, featuring the head of an elderly man and a Gothic window.

face, i.e. to his artistic representation. I have fully the same thoughts as he, but if I were expressing them I would do so in a different form and with a different language. He, however, *cannot* express himself in a different language or in a *different spirit*. Otherwise no artistic face would result.[43]

For all of his respect and even affection for Zosima as an elder, Dostoevsky denies him the freedom he accords himself as artist. Redemptive grace was to be sought not in a face but in the shape of human interactions.

In his 1930 book *The Dialectic of Myth* Aleksei Losev (1893–1988) deployed the term 'detachment' as a synonym for aesthetic disinterestedness, which he defined as the separation of a material phenomenon from its material being, its presentation as pure meaning. Opposed to this 'aesthetic detachment' is the detachment of myth, which is the presentation of phenomena separate from their meaning, in their pure materiality:

Myth [. . .] snatches things out of their ordinary course, where they are either incompatible with one another or incomprehensible or their future remains obscure, and immerses them, while preserving their reality and materiality, into another realm, where intimate connections among them are revealed, the place of each is understood, and their future destiny becomes clear.[44]

The last representative of the philosophical tradition of Solovyov, Losev links this kind of detachment to the monastic mode of existence: 'For a monk there are no indifferent things.'[45] However, it is also an option open to art: immersion in aesthetic media may renew viewers' experience of the material world as a locus of spiritual meaning. Dostoevsky saw in Optina Pustyn' a potential that was in play in Christianity but could be realized through his fiction, if he gave it space to develop.

In his recent book on Dostoevsky, Archbishop of Canterbury Rowan Williams argues that Dostoevsky's belief in the reality of the divine ground of narrative fiction does not preclude the reader's freedom to 'decide what kind of life it is desirable to live as a result of engaging with the dialogue, what is concretely made possible for him or her' as a result of this fictive engagement.[46] As Williams writes, Dostoevsky's most powerful contribution to theology is that he 'introduce[s] to the imagination a model of making that is directed toward freedom and not control' – a mode analogous to divine creation.[47] Zosima's influence is nowhere stronger than in his death: the putrefaction of his corpse demonstrates that the grace he gave was not the stardust of some otherworldly sprite, but the positive gift of a material body amid other material bodies. Zosima's death was Dostoevsky's final reckoning of the challenge issued by Holbein's painting of the dead Christ; that the creator of the world became human means that each human can become the creator (or rather the narrator) of a world.

Within the novel this animating, creative force is identified with the earthy spirit of the Karamazovs, which each of the brothers contends with in his own way. By imposing an ideological solution onto the dilemmas of injustice, and by doing so as a self-conscious author, Ivan removes himself from human dialogue and community. He spurns the lesson of his own 'Tale of the Grand Inquisitor' – where Christ responds to the Inquisitor's demagogic provocations with a simple, eloquent kiss – and refuses to embody his ethical stance in gestures of engagement. His negative responsibility for having failed to stop the murder of his own father drives him to insanity. Dmitry, for all of his failures, fully inhabits his ethical dilemmas, which are for him identified with the pouch (an 'amulet') he wears around his neck that contains the money he has borrowed from his fiancée. Representing his shame, the pouch takes the place of a cross. Like that of the good robber, crucified next to Christ, Dmitry's investment in gesture is at times obscene, but at least it is sincere.

The difference between Ivan and Dmitry is illustrated by the two brothers' reactions to their father's disgraceful 'physiognomy'. Ivan sees it as a prime example of how impossible it really is to love one's neighbour: 'In order to love a man he needs to hide; as soon as he shows his face love disappears.'[48] Like Raskolnikov, Ivan has an entire theory to justify whatever crime he finds it convenient to commit. Dmitry also finds his father's face repugnant: 'I hate his Adam's apple, his nose, his eyes, and his shameless mocking. I feel personal disgust. This is what I'm afraid of, in case I can't restrain myself . . . .'[49] As Robert Louis Jackson points out, this shows not only why Dmitry could have killed his father, but also why he did not in fact do so. Paradoxically, perhaps, Dmitry's devotion to his fleshly life and his emotions keeps him open to the action of grace: 'whether it was someone's tears, my mother interceding with God, or a radiant spirit kissing me at that instant – I don't know how, but the devil was defeated'.[50] The human form might be repulsive, but it is still the primary medium for divine intervention. When its beauty fails, its stigmata testify to the nobility of its sacrifice.

The entire problem for Alyosha, the third brother and main protagonist of the novel, is how he can unite ethical understanding with full-blooded engagement in the life of the body and soul. The process starts when Zosima tells him to leave the monastery and adopt a stance of what he calls 'active love'.[51] The process gets going when Alyosha falls to the earth and arises full of the Karamazov vital force:

> he cried in his joy even about the stars that shone to him out of the abyss, and 'he was not ashamed of this frenzy'. It was as if threads from all these countless divine worlds met at once in his soul, and it trembled, 'touching upon other worlds'.[52]

Alyosha still acknowledges Ivan's point that, 'A man's face very frequently prevents people who are still inexperienced in love from loving.'[53] In the delirium of his grief he feels himself to be at the beginning of a journey: 'And the road . . . the road is a big one, straight, radiant, crystalline, with the sun at its end . . .'.[54] Alyosha is experiencing, in Rowan Williams's words, 'the immense complexity of an embodied and embedded self, upon which countless lines of force converge'.[55] Dostoevsky's humility as an artist is expressed most directly in his refusal to draw out the destination of the forces that push out of his fictional worlds.

The author's preface to *The Brothers Karamazov* shows that the 'life story' of Aleksei Fyodorovich was to be continued in at least one further volume, dedicated to 'the life of my hero already in our time, precisely at our current moment in time'.[56] Whether or not Dostoevsky would have delivered on his intention had he lived to do so, as it stands *The Brothers Karamazov* cannot be expected to provide final answers to quandaries that animated Dostoevsky's fiction over his final fifteen years. Moreover, the unreliability of the ostensible narrator calls attention to the fantastic nature of the narration, which emerges as if hewn by many hands from a hulk of rock. It is this sculptural quality that lends the novel an air of authority, even objectivity. However, one must wonder if Dostoevsky ever really intended *The Brothers Karamazov* to provide final answers. If Dmitry and Ivan represent closed types, capable of expressing an inner idea, but incapable of the inner reformation required by life, then the author's preface insists that Alyosha is precisely an unformed self. His actions belong to the future, jutting out from the novel into extra-artistic space, that is, into the real world.

In the Preface, Dostoevsky apologizes for this rupture:

> although I call Aleksei Fyodorovich my hero, still, I myself know that he is by no means a great man [. . .] The thing is that he is a kind of agent [*deiatel'*], but an agent of an indeterminate, unclarified sort [. . .] One thing, perhaps, is rather doubtless: he is a strange man, even an eccentric. But strangeness and eccentricity will sooner harm than justify any claim to attention,

A page from a notebook relating to *The Brothers Karamazov*, with the draft of a personal letter alongside sketches of Gothic windows.

especially when everyone is striving to unite particulars and find at least some general sense in the general senselessness.[57]

Dostoevsky then declares that his hero's eccentricity to empirical reality does not exclude the possibility of his having broad significance, for

> not only is an odd man 'not always' a particular and isolated case, but, on the contrary, it sometimes happens that it is precisely he, perhaps, who bears within himself the heart of the whole, while the other people of his epoch – they have all for some reason been torn away from it for a time by some gust of wind.[58]

Faced with the problem of defining Alyosha's exceptional physiognomy, the reader is provided with the negative example of the prosecutor at Dmitry's trial, who paints the members of the Karamazov family as familiar types from Russian society: Fyodor Pavlovich is 'one of our modern-day fathers'; Ivan 'is one of our modern young men, brilliantly educated, with quite a powerful mind, who, however, no longer believes in anything, who has already scrapped and rejected much, too much in life'; Dmitry 'seems to represent ingenuous Russia [. . .] she is here, our dear mother Russia, we can smell her, we can hear her'.[59] These stereotypical characterizations are false insofar as they preclude further development on the part of the characters; but they do capture something of the characters. The prosecutor's characterization of Alyosha is false in a more fundamental sense. According to the prosecutor, Alyosha betrays 'that timid despair that leads so many in our poor society, fearing its cynicism and depravity, and mistakenly ascribing all evil to European enlightenment, to themselves, as they put it, to the "native soil"'.[60] Nothing in Alyosha justifies such a dismissive explanation of his noviciate at the monastery, but the prosecutor uses it to predict Alyosha's future membership in another Russian stereotype of 'dark mysticism on the moral side, and witless chauvinism on the civic side'.[61] In Alyosha's case the prosecutor's psychological myopia leads to utter fantasy. Alyosha's future is not only open, but its very vector remains unknown and unpredictable. It is certainly impossible to predict by the legal, causal reasoning of a grandstanding celebrity lawyer.

In his final years Dostoevsky gave increasingly frequent public readings, often for charitable causes like the Writers' Fund, which had supported him at times of need in the 1860s. In the middle of 1880 Dostoevsky interrupted work on the final books of *The Brothers Karamazov* to speak at the unveiling of a new monument to Pushkin in Moscow. Coming after a tumultuous twenty-year period of reform, terror and reaction, the Pushkin celebration was widely seen as a major step in the formation of a civil society in Russia, an open sphere of public discourse neither directed nor dominated by the state, the church or the radical intelligentsia. The conciliatory mood reached such extremes that Dostoevsky even laid aside his longstanding hostility towards Turgenev, with whom he shared centre stage.

The unveiling took place on 6 June, and the next day Dostoevsky recited the speech of the monk Pimen from Pushkin's *Boris Godunov*; annoyingly, Turgenev reaped more curtain calls for his 'most awful' recitation of more accessible verse. Still, Dostoevsky was in his element:

The reception offered me yesterday was amazing. During the intermission I went through the hall, and a horde of people, young people, grey-haired people, and ladies, rushed up to me, saying: 'You are our prophet. You have made us better since we read *The Karamazovs*.' In short, I am convinced that *The Karamazovs* has colossal significance.[62]

Dostoevsky capitalized on this expectant mood in his speech the next day, 8 June, when it was his turn to address the assembled dignitaries and press with a speech on Pushkin, about whom Dostoevsky had invariably written with the utmost affection throughout his life. The speech was so successful that Dostoevsky hurried it into print in the conservative newspaper *Moskovskie vedomosti* (Moscow News), whence it was reprinted in papers across the land; he also issued it as part of a unique issue of the *Writer's Diary* for 1880. Dostoevsky's main idea was that in his poetic narratives Pushkin had recognized the truth and necessity both of Russia's modernized and Europeanized elite and of the traditional cultural forms that it had eclipsed. To cultural conservatives Dostoevsky asserted the need for Russia to enter into world culture. To the intelligentsia Dostoevsky addressed a simple thought taken from Pushkin's 1829 narrative poem *The Gypsies*: 'Humble thyself, proud man!'[63] The second message, the one addressed to the intelligentsia, was the one that was communicated most clearly, reinforcing as it did the ascetic gesture of *The Brothers Karamazov*. Answering a congratulatory telegram, Dostoevsky again described the 'effect' of his speech: 'a multitude of people, crying, embraced each other and *swore to each other to be better in the future*, and this is not an isolated fact', Dostoevsky wrote, adding: 'this is not vainglory; it is by these instants that you live, and for them that you are born into the world.'[64] For the second time in his life Dostoevsky had ascended a stage before a crowd of expectant viewers and experienced an instant that exploded into eternity. This time it was not an execution, but a Pentecost.

Was the Pushkin speech Dostoevsky's crowning triumph or a final betrayal of his radical commitment to aesthetic form? At the close of the speech Dostoevsky declares: 'If our idea is a fantasy, then with Pushkin at least this fantasy has something to base itself on.'[65] *The Brothers Karamazov* was also intended as a kind of beachhead of the fantastic in the real world, but the speech suggested that it could not prevail without ideological reinforcement. The prophetic mantle Dostoevsky donned in his final years covered up his ailing body, but it also prevented the full shock of *The Brothers Karamazov* from being felt immediately. It is too easy to read the novel romantically. It closes with Alyosha summoning Dmitry's faith in his self-image held in his memory: 'You wanted to resurrect another man in yourself through torments; I think you should always remember this other man, for your entire life and wherever you run away to – and this will be enough for you.'[66] However, as is clear from any one of his works over his entire career, the image was never enough for Dostoevsky, if it was not capable of agency in the world. It is telling that the title of this sub-chapter in the Epilogue to *The Brothers Karamazov* is 'For a Moment the Lie Became the Truth'.

Dostoevsky's intention to provide the image of a 'positively beautiful man' had repeatedly foundered in a series of catastrophes – Raskolnikov's imprisonment for murder, Myshkin's confinement for insanity, Stavrogin's suicide in shame, and Arkady's failure as a writer in *The Adolescent*. The pilgrimage to Optina Pustyn', upon reflection, represents Dostoevsky's attempt to break out of these patterns of repetition by executing a return to his origins before literature, and beyond literature, and yet through literature.

Before taking up the continuation of *The Brothers Karamazov*, Dostoevsky decided to resume the *Writer's Diary* for 1881. Among other concerns, including tensions with European powers over Russian expansion in the Black Sea and Central Asia ('The Russian is not only a European, but also an Asian'; 'Constantinople must be ours'), the opening section of the January issue addresses the heightened public interest in economic and financial matters; Dostoevsky updates the old 'native-soil' ideology, arguing that the government should look beyond immediate fiscal considerations and prioritize 'healing the roots' of society, that is, ensuring the financial solvency of the peasantry.[67]

> After all, if only we can rid ourselves of a twentieth share of the painfully anxious attention we pay [the existing situation] every year and turn this painfully anxious attention, also in its twentieth part, to something else, then the matter will begin to seem almost non-fantastic, rather quite possible [. . .] it will transfigure itself into something completely different than now, will subordinate itself to a new principle and enter into its sense and spirit, will transfigure itself for the better, even for the very best. They'll say I am speaking in riddles, but not at all.[68]

He quotes Ivan Krylov's fable about a pig that eats the roots of the oak tree that is the source of the acorns on which it depends. Dostoevsky specifies that the St Petersburg intelligentsia – 'having isolated itself in the Finnish bog' – must regain its respect for the 'broad sea of the Russian land', the people. He reaffirms his belief that the Russia nation harbours an 'inherent' thirst for 'great, universal, all-national, all-fraternal unity in the name of Christ', which he calls 'our Russian "socialism"' and which is represented on earth by the Tsar.[69] Dostoevsky anticipates that Alexander ii's emancipation of the serfs would soon be crowned by 'an emancipation of our minds and hearts from the serf-like dependence on Europe which we have suffered for two whole centuries'.[70]

Dostoevsky's final intellectual testament went unheeded: Alexander ii was assassinated on 1 March 1881 by a group of young men from the radical terrorist organization People's Will. Dostoevsky did not live to see the death of the Tsar who had represented for him not only the regeneration of Russian society, but also his own personal re-emergence into literature after prison and exile. The new issue of the *Writer's Diary* had just been sent to the printers when on the night of 25–6 January Dostoevsky began spitting up blood from a burst artery in his diseased lungs (in addition to emphysema, he has been posthumously diagnosed with tuberculosis). Brushing the incident off, Dostoevsky went on with everyday affairs, reviewing the subscription numbers for the new *Writer's Diary*, but lunch culminated in an animated disagreement with his sister Vera about the decade-long litigation over the Kumanin estate, after which Dostoevsky was again taken ill. A team of doctors was soon joined by a priest from the nearby church, who administered last rites, and by Apollon Maikov, who bade farewell to his old friend. He breathed his last at 8:38 on the evening of 28 January 1881 and, in the words of his wife, 'passed into eternity'.[71]

Epilogue: The Convict

Even in his final repose Dostoevsky was unable to maintain the solemn dignity he so craved. In the months before his death Dostoevsky had become a public star; accordingly, his funeral became a spectacle. His widow Anna estimated that tens of thousands accompanied the funeral cortège to the cemetery of the St Alexander Nevsky Monastery in St Petersburg.[1] Some found it distasteful that the massive crowd applauded after every speaker, some of whom were obscure writers hogging the stage. Anna was delayed by the crowds and hardly made it in; lacking a ticket, she was told that 'There are a lot of Dostoevsky widows here already, some alone, some with children.'[2] Despite the crush, however, most attendees found it a touching event worthy of Dostoevsky's new status as spiritual guide to the young. Philosopher Vladimir Solovyov cut an 'apostolic figure' as he eulogized his deceased friend.[3] Among the speakers was Aleksandr Palm, who had stood with Dostoevsky before the firing squad that dark day in December 1849.

A student records that one passer-by asked who was being buried with such pomp; he was given the puzzling answer: 'A convict.'[4] The characterization was not so far from the truth. For over 30 years Dostoevsky had lived under a suspended death sentence and in the shadow of the Dead House. He had often relived the moment of his first near-death experience in epileptic fits, desperate gambles, constant writing to deadline and other

Aleksandr Rukavishnikov, Dostoevsky monument in Moscow, erected 1997.

Ivan Nikolaev, mural in Dostoevskaya metro station in Moscow.

flirtations with iron necessity. He had plotted it over and over again in his fictional works. John Middleton Murry once remarked on the 'metaphysical obscenity' of Dostoevsky's work: 'It is not that his is a cruel genius,' he argued, citing a characterization first offered by Russian critic Nikolai Mikhailovsky, 'but that he, in whom the human consciousness worked more keenly than in other men of his age, was more terribly the victim of the ultimate cruelty of things.'[5] Dostoevsky could have been reflecting on his life in art when he jotted in a notebook: 'Being only begins to be when it is threatened by non-being.'[6]

The dramatic oscillations of his life and fictions became so inscribed in his form that he has proven difficult to memorialize (no less than his contemporary Leo Tolstoy). Statues and other effigies frequently resort to copying Vasily Perov's portrait of 1872, which for Anna Dostoevskaya captured a characteristic moment of creative self-absorption before an explosion of frenzied activity. Efforts to instil some kind of movement into this impenetrable pose have led to comic effects, like the statue outside the Russian State Library in Moscow, in which Dostoevsky appears to be shifting uncomfortably in his seat. In 2009 a new metro station was named for Dostoevsky, since it serves the area in Moscow around the hospital where the writer's father had worked. Ivan Nikolaev's large murals are based on Dostoevsky's major fictions; one depicts a suicide from *Demons* and has drawn criticism for the potential harm caused by such public displays of morbidity. Thus far, then, Dostoevsky has survived all attempts to consign him to the status of a classic, defying us to join him at the edge of the possible, where danger is so easily confused with redemption.

Conceived in moments of suspended faith, Dostoevsky's fictions have proven to be supremely open to history. The philosopher Vasily Rozanov once wrote that 'every time that something uncomfortable is felt on the paths of historical life, when the nations that follow it are shaken or confused by something, the name and image of Dostoevsky will awake with undiminished power.'[7] At the same time, Rozanov argues that Dostoevsky was himself the Inquisitor, ready in the name of human freedom to flatter readers with convenient shortcuts and absolve them of responsibility. As early as 1868 this mysterious force generated fantastic rumours about Dostoevsky's own life. In *Les Mystères du palais des czars (sous l'empereur Nicolas I)*, an author hiding behind the pseudonym Paul Grimm outraged Dostoevsky by placing him at the centre of a plot against the Tsar in 1855 (when the real Dostoevsky was still serving as a private in Semipalatinsk); the novel ends with Dostoevsky in prison and his wife Natasha entering a monastery. Soon after Dostoevsky's death his friend Nikolai Strakhov began imputing to Dostoevsky the sordid crime of his character Stavrogin. From Viktor Shklovsky (1933) to Igor Volgin's *Last Year of Dostoevsky* (1986) Soviet authors were intrigued by the possibility of a link between the onset of Dostoevsky's fatal illness and the arrest that same day of a radical terrorist who lived in a neighbouring apartment. One of the most recent examples of this mythicization of Dostoevsky's life, J. M. Coetzee's *The Master of Petersburg* (1984), projects the conspiratorial atmosphere of *Demons* onto Dostoevsky's life, resulting in a weirdly compelling fiction about Dostoevsky's inner world.

The imaginative treatment of Dostoevsky's biography reflects the experience of readers who find themselves implicated in his fictions. In his review of Joseph Frank's biography, David Foster Wallace intersperses his perceptive commentary on Dostoevsky's life with painful confessions about his own tortured self-questioning. Vladimir Sorokin's play *Dostoevsky Trip* (1997) enacts a pharmaceutical anti-utopia where writers' names denote brands of psychotropic narcotics. The seven drug-addled characters take a Dostoevsky pill that propels them, *in medias res*, into a travesty of *The Idiot*. Seeing that Dostoevsky is too strong to be taken alone, chemical engineers in the drug lab decide to dilute it with some Stephen King. As

Wallace argues, Dostoevsky's fictions remain urgent to us because they continue to confront us with 'degrees of passion, conviction, and engagement with deep moral issues that we – here, today – cannot or do not permit ourselves'.[8]

References

In order to facilitate the use of any of the many worthy translations into English (or other languages, for that matter), references to Dostoevsky's works are given as numeric indices denoting their divisions. For example, 1.i.5 refers to Part 1, Book i, chapter 5 of *The Brothers Karamazov*; III.iv refers to Part III, chapter iv of *The Idiot*. In addition, reference is made to the authoritative edition of Dostoevsky's complete works in Russian (*PSS*). To ensure accuracy and consistency all translations are by the author, even when reference is made (for readers' convenience) to an English-language edition. Dates are given according to the Julian calendar, which during Dostoevsky's life ran twelve days behind the Gregorian calendar used in Western Europe; thus Dostoevsky's birthdate – 30 October 1821 – corresponds to 11 November in the European calendar. When Dostoevsky is outside of Russia, the Western European date is given.

DVS   *Dostoevskii v vospominaniiakh sovremennikov*, ed. K. Tiun'kin, 2 vols (Moscow, 1990)

DZN   *Dostoevskii v zabytykh i neizvestnykh vospominaniiakh sovremennikov*, ed. S. V. Belov (St Petersburg, 1993)

LN 83   *Neizdannyi Dostoevskii. Zapisnye knizhki i tetradi 1860–1881 gg. Literaturnoe nasledstvo*, vol. LXXXIII, ed. I. S. Zil'bershtein and L. M. Rozenblium (Moscow, 1971)

LN 86   *F. M. Dostoevskii. Novye materialy i issledovaniia. Literaturnoe nasledstvo*, vol. LXXXVI, ed. I. S. Zil'bershtein and L. M. Rozenblium (Moscow, 1973)

PSS   *Polnoe sobranie sochinenii*, F. M. Dostoevskii, 30 vols (Leningrad, 1971–90)

WD   *A Writer's Diary*, Fyodor Dostoevsky.

Introduction: Faces of Dostoevsky

1 *DVS* 1: 239.
2 Sigmund Freud, 'Dostoevsky and Parricide', in *The Standard Edition of the Complete Psychological Works*, ed. James Strachey (London, 1964), vol. XXI, p. 177.
3 Eugène-Melchior de Vogüé, *The Russian Novelists*, trans. Jane Loring Edmands (Boston, MA, 1887), p. 199; translation adjusted according to E.-M. de Vogüé, *Le Roman Russe* (Lausanne, 1971), p. 252.
4 *LN* 83: 674.
5 *The Idiot* II.ii; *PSS* 8: 167.
6 *DVS* 1: 218.
7 *DVS* 1: 172.
8 *DZN* 163.
9 *DZN* 200.
10 *DVS* 2: 139–40.
11 *DVS* 2: 145–6.
12 *WD* 1873.IX; *PSS* 21: 76.
13 Charles Olson, 'Dostoevsky and *The Possessed*', in *Collected Prose*, ed. Donald Allen and Benjamin Friedlander, introduction by Robert Creeley (Berkeley, CA, 1997), p.127.
14 *DVS* 2: 145.
15 Konstantin Barsht, *Risunki v rukopisiakh Dostoevskogo* (St Petersburg, 1994).
16 *LN* 86: 487.
17 *LN* 86: 488.
18 *DVS* 1: 381.

1 A Noble Vocation

1   *PSS* 18: 135–6.

2   *PSS* 30/1: 212.

3   Andrei Dostoevskii, *Vospominaniia* (Moscow, 1999), pp. 70, 80–81.

4   *WD* 1876.I.iii.1; *PSS* 22: 27.

5   *PSS* 28/1: 100.

6   William Mills Todd III, 'Dostoevskii as a Professional Writer', in *The Cambridge Companion to Dostoevskii*, ed. W. J. Leatherbarrow (Cambridge, 2002), pp. 66–92.

7   *PSS* 29/2: 156.

8   *PSS* 29/2: 157.

9   *PSS* 28/1: 63.

10 Igor' Volgin, *Poslednii god Dostoevskogo: Istoricheskie zapiski*, 2nd edn (Moscow, 1991), p. 197.

11 *Poor Folk*, 1 July; *PSS* 1: 59; see I. I. Lapshin, *Estetika Dostoevskogo* (Berlin, 1923), p. 53.

12 *Poor Folk*, 30 September; *PSS* 1: 106.

13 *Poor Folk*, undated letter; *PSS* 1: 108.

14 N. G. Goncharova, *F. M. Dostoevskii v zerkalakh grafiki i kritiki* (Moscow, 2005), p. 161.

15 Peter Yakovlevich Chaadayev, *Philosophical Letters and Apology of a Madman*, trans. and introduction by Mary-Barbara Zeldin (Knoxville, TN, 1969), pp. 35–6.

16 *PSS* 28/1: 106–7.

17 *PSS* 28/1: 134.

18 *PSS* 28/1: 137–8.

19 *PSS* 28/1: 139.

20 *Notes from Underground* I.ii; *PSS* 5: 101.

21 *The Double* I; *PSS* 1: 110.

22 *The Double* I; *PSS* 1: 113.

23 *The Double* VI; *PSS* 1: 147.

24 Goncharova, *F. M. Dostoevskii*, p. 162.

25 *PSS* 28/1: 139.

26 *White Nights*, 1st Night; *PSS* 2: 102.

27 *White Nights*, 1st Night; *PSS* 2: 103.

28 Joseph Frank, *Dostoevsky: The Seeds of Revolt, 1821–1849* (Princeton, NJ,

1977), p. 346.
29 *White Nights*, 1st Night; *pss* 2: 107.
30 *White Nights*, 1st Night; *pss* 2: 109.
31 *White Nights*, 2nd Night; *pss* 2: 111.
32 *White Nights*, 2nd Night; *pss* 2: 112–13.
33 *White Nights*, 2nd Night; *pss* 2: 112.
34 *The Idiot* iii.iv; *pss* 8: 327.
35 *White Nights*, 2nd Night; *pss* 2: 114.
36 *White Nights*, 2nd Night; *pss* 2: 115–16.
37 *White Nights*, 2nd Night; *pss* 2: 116.
38 *White Nights*, 2nd Night; *pss* 2: 118.
39 *White Nights*, 2nd Night; *pss* 2: 125.
40 *White Nights*, 2nd Night; *pss* 2: 127.
41 *White Nights*, 3rd Night; *pss* 2: 137.
42 *White Nights*, 4th Night; *pss* 2: 140.
43 *White Nights*, 4th Night; *pss* 2: 141.
44 *pss* 16: 10.
45 Konstantin Barsht, *Risunki v rukopisiakh Dostoevskogo* (St Petersburg, 1994), p. 187.
46 *pss* 28/1: 126.
47 *pss* 30/1: 203.
48 *pss* 28/1: 116.
49 *pss* 28/1: 155.

2 Ten Years of Silence

1 *pss* 18: 174.
2 *pss* 18: 180.
3 Vissarion Belinsky, 'Letter to Gogol', in *Russian Philosophy*, ed. James M. Edie, James P. Scanlan and Mary-Barbara Zeldin, 3 vols (Chicago, il, 1965), vol. i, p. 314.
4 *pss* 18: 192.
5 *pss* 18: 133.
6 *pss* 18: 127–8.
7 *pss* 18: 123–4, 125.
8 *pss* 18: 126.

9   *PSS* 18: 128–9.

10 *PSS* 18: 120, 126.

11 *PSS* 2: 282.

12 *PSS* 2: 295.

13 *PSS* 28/1: 164, 166.

14 *White Nights*, 2nd Night; *PSS* 2: 118.

15 *PSS* 2: 430.

16 Vyacheslav Ivanov, *Freedom and the Tragic Life: A Study in Dostoevsky* (New York, 1952), p. 37.

17 Jacques Derrida, 'Demeure: Fiction and Testimony', in Maurice Blanchot, *The Instant of My Death*, trans. Elizabeth Rottenberg (Stanford, CA, 2000), p. 55. Derrida was writing about Maurice Blanchot's brief text 'The Instant of My Death'.

18 *DVS* 1: 337.

19 *PSS* 28/1: 169.

20 *PSS* 28/1: 177.

21 *PSS* 28/1: 171.

22 *PSS* 28/1: 181.

23 *PSS* 28/1: 172

24 *PSS* 28/1: 171.

25 *PSS* 28/2: 115.

26 *DVS* 1: 347–8.

27 *PSS* 29/1: 145.

28 *PSS* 2: 409.

29 See Irina Kirillova, 'Dostoevsky's Markings in the Gospel According to St John', in *Dostoevsky and the Christian Tradition*, ed. George Pattison and Diane Oenning Thompson (Cambridge, 2001), pp. 41–50.

30 *PSS* 28/1: 176.

31 *PSS* 28/1: 322.

32 'Uncle's Dream' xv; *PSS* 2: 392.

33 *The Village Stepanchikovo* II.vi; *PSS* 3: 161.

34 *PSS* 28/1: 216.

35 *The Village Stepanchikovo* I.i; *PSS* 3: 7.

36 *PSS* 28/1: 346.

3 The Name

1 *PSS* 28/1: 337

2 *PSS* 28/1: 335.

3 *PSS* 28/1: 340.

4 *PSS* 28/1: 349.

5 *PSS* 28/1: 351.

6 *PSS* 18: 35.

7 *PSS* 18: 36.

8 *PSS* 18: 36–7.

9 *PSS* 18: 39.

10 *PSS* 28/2: 29.

11 *PSS* 28/2: 61

12 *PSS* 28/2: 73.

13 *PSS* 28/2: 66.

14 *PSS* 28/2: 50.

15 *The Insulted and the Injured* II.x; *PSS* 3: 291.

16 *PSS* 20: 134–5.

17 *The Insulted and the Injured* I.xii; *PSS* 3: 218–19.

18 *The Insulted and the Injured* II.v; *PSS* 3: 265.

19 *The Insulted and the Injured* II.xi; *PSS* 3: 294.

20 *The Insulted and the Injured* I.viii; *PSS* 3: 200

21 *The Insulted and the Injured* I.ix; *PSS* 3: 202.

22 *The Insulted and the Injured* I.viii; *PSS* 3: 197.

23 *The Insulted and the Injured* III.ii; *PSS* 3: 310.

24 *The Insulted and the Injured* I.x; *PSS* 3: 208.

25 *The Insulted and the Injured* II.iii; *PSS* 3: 255.

26 *The Insulted and the Injured* II.i; *PSS* 3: 240.

27 *The Insulted and the Injured* II.xi; *PSS* 3: 300.

28 *The Insulted and the Injured* II.v; *PSS* 3: 266.

29 *The Insulted and the Injured* II.xi; *PSS* 3: 296; cf. 325.

30 *PSS* 28/1: 207.

31 *Notes from the Dead House* I.Introduction; *PSS* 4: 8.

32 *Notes from the Dead House* II.iii; *PSS* 4: 154–5.

33 *Notes from the Dead House* I.i; *PSS* 4: 10.

34 Roland Barthes, *Writing Degree Zero*, trans. Annette Lavers and Colin Smith, preface by Susan Sontag (New York, 1968).

35 *Notes from the Dead House* I.i; *PSS* 4: 9.

36 *Notes from the Dead House* I.xi; *PSS* 4: 122–3.

37 *Notes from the Dead House* I.xi; *PSS* 4:130.

38 *Notes from the Dead House* II.i; *PSS* 4: 140.

39 *Notes from the Dead House* II.i; *PSS* 4: 140.

4 The Wager

1 *Winter Notes on Summer Impressions* V; *PSS* 5: 69.

2 Nikolai Chernyshevsky, *What Is to Be Done?*, trans. Michael R. Katz (Ithaca, NY, and London, 1989), p. 376.

3 Karl Marx and Friedrich Engels, *The Communist Manifesto: A Modern Edition*, introduction by Eric Hobsbawm (London and New York, 1998), p. 37.

4 *PSS* 18: 50.

5 See Robert Louis Jackson, *The Art of Dostoevsky: Deliriums and Nocturnes* (Princeton, NJ, 1981); see also Jackson, *Dostoevsky's Quest for Form: A Study of His Philosophy of Art*, 2nd edn (n.p., 1978).

6 *PSS* 18: 78.

7 *PSS* 18: 78.

8 Walter Pater, *The Renaissance*, ed. Donald L. Hill (Berkeley, CA, 1980), p. 190.

9 See, for instance, the unsigned article 'Nashi domashnie dela. Sovremennye zametki', *Vremia*, VII (July 1861), 4th pagination, pp. 17–18.

10 Jackson, *The Art of Dostoevsky*, p. 170.

11 Joseph Frank, *Dostoevsky: The Stir of Liberation, 1860–1865* (Princeton, NJ, 1986), p. 316.

12 Chernyshevsky, *What Is to Be Done?*, p. 48.

13 Ibid., p. 49.

14 *PSS* 28/2: 34.

15 *PSS* 28/2: 405.

16 *PSS* 28/2: 73.

17 *PSS* 5: 342.

18 *PSS* 28/1: 85.

19 *PSS* 28/2: 70.

20 *PSS* 28/2: 121.

21 Frank, *Dostoevsky: The Stir of Liberation,* p. 263.

22 *PSS* 5: 382.

23 *PSS* 5: 379.

24 *PSS* 28/2: 116.

25 *PSS* 20: 172–5.

26 On the media sources of Dostoevsky's novels see: Konstantine Klioutchkine, 'The Rise of *Crime and Punishment* from the Air of the Media', *Slavic Review,* LXI/1 (Spring 2002), pp. 88–108; Anne Lounsbery, 'Print Culture and Real Life in Dostoevskii's *Demons*', *Dostoevsky Studies,* n.s. XI (2007), pp. 25–37.

27 Mikhail Bakhtin, *Problems of Dostoevsky's Poetics,* ed. and trans. Caryl Emerson, introduction by Wayne C. Booth (Minneapolis, MN, 1984), p. 232.

28 Gary Saul Morson, *Narrative and Freedom: The Shadows of Time* (New Haven, CT, and London, 1994), p. 38.

29 *PSS* 5: 99.

30 *PSS* 14: 5.

5 In Suspense

1 *PSS* 28/2: 119.

2 *PSS* 28/2: 119.

3 *PSS* 28/2: 120.

4 *PSS* 28/2: 108.

5 *PSS* 28/2: 127.

6 *PSS* 28/2: 120.

7 *PSS* 28/2: 132.

8 *PSS* 28/2: 130.

9 *PSS* 28/2: 138.

10 *PSS* 28/2: 151.

11 *PSS* 28/2: 158.

12 *PSS* 28/2: 150.

13 *PSS* 28/2: 154.

14 *PSS* 28/2: 155.

15 E.-M. de Vogüé, *The Russian Novelists,* trans. Jane Loring Edmands (Boston, MA, 1887), p. 184.

16 *PSS* 28/2: 160.

17 *PSS* 6: 422.

18 *PSS* 7: 154–5.

19 *Crime and Punishment* ii.vi; *PSS* 6: 130.

20 *Crime and Punishment* ii.vi; *PSS* 6: 130.

21 *Crime and Punishment* i.ii; *PSS* 6: 25.

22 *Crime and Punishment* i.v; *PSS* 5: 50; *Crime and Punishment* i.vi; *PSS* 5: 55.

23 *Crime and Punishment* i.vii; *PSS* 6: 65.

24 *PSS* 6: 421.

25 *Crime and Punishment* iv.iv.

26 *Crime and Punishment* v.iv; *PSS* 6: 311.

27 *Crime and Punishment* v.iv; *PSS* 6: 314.

28 *Crime and Punishment* v.iv; *PSS* 6: 315.

29 *Crime and Punishment* vi.viii; *PSS* 6: 403.

30 *Crime and Punishment* vi.viii; *PSS* 6: 410.

31 Gary Saul Morson, 'Introduction', in Fyodor Dostoevsky, *The Gambler* (New York, 2003), p. xxiii.

32 Walter Benjamin, *Illuminations*, trans. Harry Zohn, ed. and introduction by Hannah Arendt (New York, 1968), p. 100.

33 Roland Barthes, *s/z: An Essay*, trans. Richard Howard (New York, 1974), p. 29.

34 Ibid., p. 217.

35 *PSS* 29/1: 225

36 Nikolai Punin, *Mir svetel liubov'iu. Dnevniki. Pis'ma* (Moscow, 2000), p. 373.

37 Marcel Proust, *Remembrance of Things Past*, trans. C. I. Scott Moncrieff and Terence Kilmartin (New York, 1982), vol. iii, p. 386.

38 Fernand Léger, *Functions of Painting* (New York, 1973), p. 65.

39 Vladimir Nizhny, *Lessons with Eisenstein*, trans. and ed. Ivor Montagu and Jay Leyda (London, 1962), p. 97.

40 Karla Oeler, *A Grammar of Murder: Violent Scenes and Film Form* (Chicago, il, 2009), p. 38.

41 Andrei Tarkovsky, *Time within Time: The Diaries, 1970–1986*, trans. Kitty Hunter-Blair (London and Boston, ma, 1994), p. 84; the quoted phrase is missing in the fuller Russian-language edition: Andrei Tarkovskii, *Martirolog: Dnevniki 1970–1986* (n.p., 2008), p. 106.

42 Andrei Tarkovsky, *Sculpting in Time*, trans. Kitty Hunter-Blair (Austin,

TX, 1984), pp. 25, 74; translation adjusted according to Andrei
Tarkovskii, *Arkhivy. Dokumenty. Vospominaniia*, ed. P. D. Volkova
(Moscow, 2002), pp. 119, 175–6.

43 Robert Bresson, *Notes on the Cinematographer* (Copenhagen, 1997), p. 124.

44 Paul Schrader, 'Robert Bresson, Possibly', *Robert Bresson*, ed. James
Quandt (Toronto, 1998), p. 488. This volume also contains
considerations of Dostoevsky and Bresson by T. Jefferson Kline and
Mireille Latil le Dantec.

45 Brian Price, *Neither God nor Master: Robert Bresson and Radical Politics*
(Minneapolis, MN, 2011), p. 106.

46 Jean-Paul Sartre, 'Why Write?', in *What Is Literature? and Other Essays*,
introduction by Steven Ungar (Cambridge, MA, 1988), p. 63.

47 Ibid., pp. 50, 53, 57–8.

48 Ibid., p. 61.

49 Ibid., p. 67.

50 Ibid., p. 69.

51 Giorgio Agamben, *The Man Without Content*, trans. Georgia Albert
(Stanford, CA, 1994), p. 114.

6 Dreams and Demons

1 *PSS* 28/2: 453.

2 *PSS* 28/2: 205.

3 *The Idiot*, Epilogue; *PSS* 8: 510.

4 *The Adolescent* III.vii.2; *PSS* 13: 375.

5 *The Adolescent* III.vii.2; *PSS* 13: 377.

6 Anna Grigor'evna Dostoevskaia, *Dnevnik 1867 goda*, ed. S. V.
Zhitomirskaia (Moscow, 1993), p. 103.

7 *PSS* 28/2: 277.

8 Anna Dostoevsky, *Dostoevsky: Reminiscences*, trans. and ed. Beatrice
Stillman, introduction by Helen Muchnic (New York, 1975), p. 134.

9 *The Idiot* III.vi; *PSS* 8: 339.

10 *The Idiot* II.x; *PSS* 8: 246.

11 Dostoevskaia, *Dnevnik 1867 goda*, p. 388.

12 *PSS* 28/2: 241.

13 Aleksei Remizov, *Ogon' veshchei: Sny i predson'e*, ed. E. R. Obatnina (St

Petersburg, 2005), p. 284.

14 *The Idiot* II.v; *PSS* 8: 188–9.

15 *The Idiot* II.ii; *PSS* 8: 168.

16 *The Idiot* II.ii; *PSS* 8: 167.

17 *The Idiot* II.xi; *PSS* 8: 254.

18 *The Idiot* III.iv; *PSS* 8: 311.

19 *The Idiot* III.v, vi; *PSS* 8: 328, 340.

20 *The Idiot* III.vii; *PSS* 8: 345.

21 *The Idiot* II.v; *PSS* 8: 193–4.

22 *The Idiot* II.v; *PSS* 8: 195.

23 *The Idiot* III.x; *PSS* 8: 381; see Remizov, *Ogon' veshchei*, p. 302.

24 *PSS* 28/2 251.

25 *The Idiot* II.ii; *PSS* 8: 283.

26 *The Idiot* IV.vi; *PSS* 8: 436.

27 *The Idiot* III.ii; *PSS* 8: 287.

28 *The Idiot* IV.xi; *PSS* 8: 508.

29 Viacheslav Ivanov, *Sobranie sochinenii* (Brussels, 1971–86), vol. IV, p.
    428; cf. Ivanov, *Freedom and the Tragic Life: A Study in Dostoevsky* (New
    York, 1952), p. 41.

30 *The Idiot* III.vi; *PSS* 8: 339.

31 Julia Kristeva, *Black Sun: Depression and Melancholia*, trans. Leon S.
    Roudiez (New York, 1989), pp. 217.

32 *PSS* 29/1: 88.

33 *PSS* 29/1: 115.

34 *PSS* 29/1: 115.

35 *PSS* 28/2: 329.

36 *PSS* 29/1: 112.

37 *PSS* 29/1: 145.

38 *PSS* 29/1: 136.

39 *PSS* 29/1: 172.

40 Anne Lounsbery, 'Print Culture and Real Life in Dostoevsky's
    Demons', *Dostoevsky Studies*, n.s. XI (2007), pp. 25–37: p. 36.

41 Ibid., p. 30.

42 See W. J. Leatherbarrow, '*The Devils* in the Context of Dostoevsky's
    Life and Works', *The Devils: A Critical Companion*, ed. W. J.
    Leatherbarrow (Evanston, IL, 1999), p. 6.

43 Vladimir Alexandrov, 'The Narrator as Author in Dostoevskij's *Besy*',

Russian Literature, XV (1984), p. 253.

44 Michael Holquist, *Dostoevsky and the Novel* (Princeton, NJ, 1977), p. 135.

45 *Demons* I.i.3; *PSS* 10: 16.

46 *Demons* II.viii; *PSS* 10: 325.

47 Joseph Frank, *Dostoevsky: The Miraculous Years, 1865–1871* (Princeton, NJ, 1995), p. 478.

48 *Demons* II.i.2; *PSS* 10: 172.

49 *PSS* 29/1: 142.

50 René Girard, *Deceit, Desire and the Novel: Self and Other in Literary Structure*, trans. Yvonne Freccero (Baltimore and London, 1965), p. 295.

51 Cited by Robert Louis Jackson, *Dostoevsky's Quest for Form*, 2nd edn (n.p., 1978), pp. 106–7.

52 Iurii Lotman, 'The Tradition Generated by *Onegin*', in *Russian Views of Pushkin's 'Eugene Onegin'*, trans. Sona Stephen Hoisington (Bloomington and Indianapolis, IN, 1988), p. 177; Iu. M. Lotman, *Pushkin* (St Petersburg, 1995), p. 462.

53 Donald Fanger, *Dostoevsky and Romantic Realism: A Study of Dostoevsky in Relation to Balzac, Dickens, and Gogol* (Evanston, IL, 1998), p. 216; cf. Jackson, *Dostoevsky's Quest for Form*, p. 109.

54 Fanger, *Dostoevsky and Romantic Realism*, p. 217.

55 Ibid., p. 264.

56 Hannah Arendt, *Reflections on Literature and Culture*, ed. and introduction by Susannah Young-ah Gottlieb (Stanford, CA, 2007), p. 279.

57 Charles Olson, 'Dostoevsky and *The Possessed*', in *Collected Prose*, ed. Donald Allen and Benjamin Friedlander, introduction by Robert Creeley (Berkeley, CA, 1997), p. 130.

58 *Demons* III.viii; *PSS* 10: 516.

59 *PSS* 11: 16.

60 J. M. Coetzee, 'Confession and Double Thoughts: Tolstoy, Rousseau, Dostoevsky', *Comparative Literature*, XXXVII (1985), pp. 193–232: p. 229.

61 *The Idiot* I.v; *PSS* 8: 54.

62 *The Idiot* I.v; *PSS* 8: 54.

63 *PSS* 28/1: 51.

7 Gestures of Engagement

1 *PSS* 28/1: 280–81.

2 *PSS* 29/1: 262.

3 *PSS* 22: 183.

4 *Demons* I.iv.2; *PSS* 10: 104.

5 *PSS* 29/1: 115.

6 *WD* 1873.III; *PSS* 21: 18.

7 *WD* 1873.III; *PSS* 21: 18.

8 *WD* 1873.V; *PSS* 21: 34.

9 *WD* 1873.V, *PSS* 21: 40.

10 *WD* 1873.V; *PSS* 21: 36.

11 *WD* 1873.V; *PSS* 21: 40.

12 *WD* 1873.V; *PSS* 21: 40.

13 *WD* 1873.IX; *PSS* 21: 73.

14 *WD* 1873.IX; *PSS* 21: 75.

15 *WD* 1873.IX; *PSS* 21: 76.

16 *WD* 1873.IX; *PSS* 21: 74.

17 *WD* 1873.IX; *PSS* 21: 77.

18 *WD* 1873.IX; *PSS* 21: 77.

19 Quoted from *Letopis' zhizni i tvorchestva F. M. Dostoevskogo, 1821–1881*, 3 vols (St Petersburg, 1993–5), vol. III, p. 23.

20 *The Adolescent* I.i.8; *PSS* 13: 17.

21 *The Adolescent* I.v.1; *PSS* 13: 66.

22 *The Adolescent* I.i.3; *PSS* 13: 7.

23 *The Adolescent* I.i.1; *PSS* 13: 5.

24 *The Adolescent* I.v.3; *PSS* 13: 72.

25 *The Adolescent* I.i.2; *PSS* 13: 6.

26 *The Adolescent* I.ii.2: *PSS* 13: 22.

27 *The Adolescent* I.i.8; *PSS* 13: 17.

28 *The Adolescent* I.vi.3; *PSS* 13: 92.

29 *The Adolescent* III.i.3; *PSS* 13: 290.

30 *The Adolescent* I.v.3; *PSS* 13: 74.

31 *The Adolescent* I.vi.2; *PSS* 13: 89.

32 *The Adolescent* I.iv.3; *PSS* 13: 63, 62.

33 *The Adolescent* I.vi.1; *PSS* 13: 82.

34 *The Adolescent* III.x.2; *PSS* 13: 407.

35 *The Adolescent* III.x.2; *PSS* 13: 408.

36 *The Adolescent* III.x.2; *PSS* 13: 409.

37 *The Adolescent* III.x.4; *PSS* 13: 413.

38 *The Adolescent* III.vii.1; *PSS* 13: 369.

39 *The Adolescent* III.vii.1; *PSS* 13: 370.

40 *The Adolescent* I.v.4; *PSS* 13: 81.

41 *The Adolescent* III.i.3; *PSS* 13: 291.

42 *The Adolescent* III.ii.4; *PSS* 13: 305.

43 *The Adolescent* III.ii.5; *PSS* 13: 306, 307.

44 *The Adolescent* III.xiii.1; *PSS* 13: 446–7.

45 *The Adolescent* III.xiii.3; *PSS* 13: 453.

46 *The Adolescent* III.xiii.3; *PSS* 13: 454.

47 *The Adolescent* III.xiii.3; *PSS* 13: 455.

48 *The Adolescent* III.xiii.3; *PSS* 13: 455.

49 *The Adolescent* III.xiii.3; *PSS* 13: 455.

50 *PSS* 16: 329.

51 *WD* 1876.I.iii; *PSS* 23: 48.

52 *WD* 1876.I.ii; *PSS* 23: 45.

53 *WD* 1876.I.iii; *PSS* 23: 46–7.

54 Robert Louis Jackson, *The Art of Dostoevsky: Deliriums and Nocturnes* (Princeton, NJ, 1981), p. 30.

55 *WD* 1876.X.iii; *PSS* 23: 144–5.

56 *WD* 1876.XI.ii.4; *PSS* 24: 33.

57 *PSS* 29/2: 78.

58 *PSS* 30/1: 8.

59 *PSS* 30/1: 9.

8 Pilgrimage

1 *PSS* 30/1: 107; *PSS* 18: 53.

2 *PSS* 29/2: 95.

3 *PSS* 29/2: 45.

4 *PSS* 30/1: 97.

5 *PSS* 29/1: 333.

6 *PSS* 30/1: 98.

7 *WD* 1877.VII–VIII.1; *PSS* 25: 172.

8 *WD* 1877.VII–VIII.ii; *PSS* 25: 180–81.

9 *PSS* 30/1: 109.

10 Aleksei Khomiakov and Ivan Kireevsky, *On Spiritual Unity: A Slavophile Anthology*, trans. and ed. Robert Bird and Boris Jakim (Hudson, NY, 1998).

11 *PSS* 29/1: 146–7.

12 *PSS* 29/1: 118.

13 I. D. Iakubovich, 'K kharakteristike stilizatsii v "Podrostke"', in *Dostoevskii: Issledovaniia i materialy*, vol. III (St Petersburg, 1978), pp. 136–43.

14 Anna Dostoevsky, *Dostoevsky: Reminiscences*, trans. and ed. Beatrice Stillman, introduction by Helen Muchnic (New York, 1975), p. 327.

15 *PSS* 28/1: 69.

16 Konstantin Leont'ev, *Zapiski otshel'nika* (Moscow, 1992), p. 415; cf. Konstantin Leontiev, *Against the Current: Selections from the Novels, Essays, Notes, and Letters*, trans. George Reavey, ed., introduction and notes by George Ivask (New York, 1969), pp. 242–4. Cf. also Margaret Ziolkowski, 'Dostoevsky and the Kenotic Tradition', in *Dostoevsky and the Christian Tradition*, ed. George Pattison and Diane Oenning Thompson (Cambridge, 2001), pp. 31–40.

17 Inok Parfenii, *Skazanie o stranstvii i puteshestvii po Rossii, Moldavii, Turtsii i Sviatoi Zemle*, 2 vols (Moscow, 2008), vol. I, pp. 222–3.

18 V. S. Solov'ev, *Sobranie sochinenii* (St Petersburg, 1901–3), vol. II, p. i.

19 Ibid., vol. II, p. iv.

20 *PSS* 30/1: 16.

21 *PSS* 30/1: 14–15.

22 *The Idiot* I.xi; *PSS* 8: 106.

23 Susan McReynolds, *Redemption and the Merchant God: Dostoevsky's Economy of Salvation and Antisemitism* (Evanston, IL, 2008).

24 Anna Dostoevsky, *Dostoevsky: Reminiscences*, p. 294.

25 *The Brothers Karamazov* I.i.5; *PSS* 14: 26

26 John Climacus, *The Ladder of Divine Ascent*, trans. Colm Luibheid and Norman Russell (New York, 1982), pp. 82–3.

27 *LN* 83: 682.

28 *PSS* 28/1: 176.

29 *PSS* 30/1: 41.

30 *PSS* 28/2 251.

31 McReynolds, *Redemption and the Merchant God*, p. 7.

32 *WD* 1877.III.ii.1; *PSS* 25: 75.

33 *WD* 1877.III.ii.2; *PSS* 25: 81.

34 *WD* 1877.III.iii.1; *PSS* 25: 90.

35 *WD* 1877.III.iii.2; *PSS* 25: 90–91.

36 *WD* 1877.III.ii.4; *PSS* 25: 87.

37 *WD* 1877.IV.i.1; *PSS* 25: 95.

38 *WD* 1877.IV.i.2; *PSS* 25: 98.

39 *WD* 1877.IV.i.3; *PSS* 25: 102.

40 *WD* 1877.IV.ii.5; *PSS* 25: 116.

41 *PSS* 29/1: 128–9.

42 *PSS* 28/1: 63.

43 *PSS* 30/1: 102.

44 Aleksei Fyodorovich Losev, *The Dialectics of Myth*, trans. Vladimir
    Marchenkov (London, 2003), p. 65.

45 Ibid., p. 139.

46 Rowan Williams, *Dostoevsky: Language, Faith and Fiction* (Waco, TX,
    2008), p. 215.

47 Ibid., p. 234.

48 *The Brothers Karamazov* II.v.4; *PSS* 14: 215.

49 *The Brothers Karamazov* III.viii.4; *PSS* 14: 355.

50 *The Brothers Karamazov* III.ix.5; *PSS* 14: 426.

51 *The Brothers Karamazov* I.ii.4; *PSS* 14: 54

52 *The Brothers Karamazov* III.vii.4; *PSS* 14: 328.

53 *The Brothers Karamazov* II.v.4; *PSS* 14: 216.

54 *The Brothers Karamazov* III.vii.4; *PSS* 14: 326.

55 Williams, *Dostoevsky*, p. 221.

56 *PSS* 14: 6.

57 *PSS* 14: 5.

58 Ibid.

59 *The Brothers Karamazov* IV.xii.6; *PSS* 15: 126; *The Brothers Karamazov*
    IV.xii.6; *PSS* 15: 128.

60 *The Brothers Karamazov* IV.xii.6; *PSS* 15: 127.

61 *The Brothers Karamazov* IV.xii.6; *PSS* 15: 127.

62 *PSS* 30/1: 182.

63 *WD* 1880.VIII.ii; *PSS* 26: 139.

64 *PSS* 30/1: 187, 188.

65 *WD* 1880.VIII.ii; *PSS* 26: 148.

66 *The Brothers Karamazov* Epilogue.ii; *PSS* 15: 185.

67 *WD* 1881.II.iii, iv; *PSS* 27: 33, 39.

68 *WD* 1881.I.iii; *PSS* 27: 14.

69 *WD* 1881.I.iv; *PSS* 27: 17, 19.

70 *WD* 1881.I.v; *PSS* 27: 25.

71 Anna Dostoevsky, *Dostoevsky: Reminiscences*.

Epilogue: The Convict

1 Anna Grigor'evna Dostoevskaia, *Dnevnik 1867 goda*, ed. S. V. Zhitomirskaia (Moscow, 1993), p. 288.

2 Anna Dostoevsky, *Dostoevsky: Reminiscences*, trans. and ed. Beatrice Stillman, introduction by Helen Muchnic (New York, 1975), p. 360.

3 *DVS* 478.

4 *DVS* 2: 483.

5 John Middleton Murry, *Fyodor Dostoevsky: A Critical Study* (London, 1916), p. 37.

6 *LN* 83: 618.

7 V. V. Rozanov, *Nesovmestimye kontrasty zhitiia: Literaturno-esteticheskie raboty raznykh let* (Moscow, 1990), p. 62.

8 David Foster Wallace, *Consider the Lobster and Other Essays* (New York and Boston, MA, 2005), p. 271.

Select Bibliography

Major Works by Dostovesky

Bednye liudi (Poor Folk, 1846)
Dvoinik (The Double, 1846)
Belye nochi (White Nights, 1848)
Selo Stepanchikovo i ego obitateli (The Village Stepanchikovo and its
    Inhabitants, 1859)
Unizhennye i oskorblennye (The Insulted and the Injured, 1861)
Zapiski iz mertvogo doma (Notes from the Dead House, 1860–61)
Zimnie zapiski o letnikh vpechatleniiakh (Winter Notes on Summer
    Impressions, 1863)
Zapiski iz podpol'ia (Notes from Underground, 1864)
Prestuplenie i nakazanie (Crime and Punishment, 1866)
Igrok (The Gambler, 1866)
Idiot (The Idiot, 1868)
Vechnyi muzh (The Eternal Husband, 1870)
Besy (Demons, 1871–2)
Dnevnik pisatelia (Writer's Diary, 1873, 1876–7, 1880, 1881)
Podrostok (The Adolescent / Raw Youth, 1875)
Brat'ia Karamazovy (The Brothers Karamazov, 1879–80)

Suggested Translations

A Writer's Diary, 2 vols, trans. Kenneth Lantz, introduction by Gary Saul
    Morson (Evanston, IL, 1993)
The Adolescent, trans. Richard Pevear and Larissa Volokhonsky (New York, 2003)
Crime and Punishment, trans. Richard Pevear and Larissa Volokhonsky
    (New York, 1992)
Demons, trans. Richard Pevear and Larissa Volokhonsky (New York, 1995)
Devils, trans. Michael R. Katz (New York, 2000)
Memoirs from the House of the Dead, trans. Jesse Coulson, ed. Ronald
    Hingley (London, 1983)
Notes from Underground, trans. Richard Pevear and Larissa Volokhonsky
    (New York, 1993)
Notes from Underground, trans. Boris Jakim (Grand Rapids, MI, 2009)
Poor Folk, trans. Robert Dessaix (Ann Arbor, MI, 1982)
Poor People, trans. Hugh Aplin (London, 2002)
The Brothers Karamazov, trans. Richard Pevear and Larissa Volokhonsky
    (San Francisco, CA, 1990)
The Brothers Karamazov, trans. Constance Garnett, revd Ralph Matlaw and
    Susan McReynolds Oddo, ed. Susan McReynolds Oddo (New York,
    2011)
The Double, trans. Hugh Aplin (London, 2004)
The Double; The Gambler, trans. Richard Pevear and Larissa Volokhonsky
    (New York, 2005)
The Eternal Husband and Other Stories, trans. Richard Pevear and Larissa
    Volokhonsky (New York, 1997)
The Eternal Husband, trans. Hugh Aplin (London, 2007)
The Gambler, trans. Hugh Aplin (London, 2006)
The Idiot, trans. Alan Myers (Oxford, 1992)
The Idiot, trans. Richard Pevear and Larissa Volokhonsky (New York, 2002)
The Insulted and Injured, trans. Boris Jakim (Grand Rapids, MI, 2011)
The Village of Stepanchikovo and its Inhabitants, trans. Ignat Avsey, revd edn
    (London, 1995)
White Nights. The Gentle Creature. The Dream of a Ridiculous Man, trans.
    Alan Myers (Oxford, 1999)
Winter Notes on Summer Impressions, trans. David Patterson (Evanston, IL,
    1997)

Further Reading

The best and most complete biography (expanding to the status of a condensed history of nineteenth-century Russian culture) is Joseph Frank's *Dostoevsky* in five volumes (Princeton, NJ, 1977–2002). A one-volume abridgement is now available as *Dostoevsky: A Writer in his Time* (Princeton, NJ, 2010).

The best place to start for interpretations of Dostoevsky's works remains Robert Louis Jackson's classic *The Art of Dostoevsky* (Princeton, NJ, 1981), especially when read alongside other classical analyses, such as Richard Peace's *Dostoevsky: An Examination of the Major Novels* (Cambridge, 1971) and Michael Holquist's *Dostoevsky and the Novel* (Princeton, NJ, 1977). For more on the philosophical aspects of Dostoevsky's writings see Jackson's *Dostoevsky's Quest for Form: A Study of his Philosophy of Art*, 2nd edn (Pittsburgh, PA, 1978) and James P. Scanlan's *Dostoevsky the Thinker* (Ithaca, NY, and London, 2002).

The often-overlooked *A Writer's Diary* rewards close reading, especially in Kenneth Lantz's translation (1995, in two volumes). A classic study of its innovative poetics is Gary Saul Morson, *The Boundaries of Genre* (Austin, TX, 1981). For a more recent study of important issues in the *Writer's Diary* see Irina Paperno, *Suicide as a Cultural Institution in Dostoevsky's Russia* (Ithaca, NY, and London, 1997).

Dostoevsky's significance for religion has recently attracted renewed attention. See *Dostoevsky and the Christian Tradition*, ed. George Pattison and Diane Oenning Thompson (Cambridge, 2001); Harriet Murav, *Holy Foolishness: Dostoevsky's Novels and the Poetics of Cultural Critique* (Stanford, CA, 1992); Steven Cassedy, *Dostoevsky's Religion* (Stanford, CA, 2005) and Susan McReynolds, *Redemption and the Merchant God: Dostoevsky's Economy of Salvation and Antisemitism* (Evanston, IL, 2008). The best single place to start is Rowan Williams, *Dostoevsky: Language, Faith and Fiction* (Waco, TX, 2008).

The Russian religious philosophers of the early twentieth century left a great deal of fascinating and influential work on Dostoevsky; see especially Vasily Rozanov, *Dostoevsky and the Legend of the Grand Inquisitor*, trans. Spencer Roberts (Ithaca, NY, 1972); Vyacheslav Ivanov, *Freedom and the Tragic Life:*

A Study in Dostoevsky (New York, 1952) and Nikolai Berdyaev, *Dostoevsky*, trans. Donald Attwater (New York, 1957). Western European writers were also among Dostoevsky's most sensitive readers; see John Middleton Murry's *Fyodor Dostoevsky: A Critical Study* (London, 1916) and André Gide's *Dostoevsky* (London, 1925).

Acknowledgements

I would like to thank the many students with whom I have been fortunate to read Dostoevsky at the University of Chicago, and who have done so much to shape the way I understand his works. I have received valuable assistance in my work from many colleagues, including Konstantin Barsht, Adrian Guiu, Natalya Anatolyevna Kostina, Konstantin Lappo-Danilevskii, Oleg Marchenko, Susan McReynolds, Claire Roosien and Davide Stimilli. For help with the images I am grateful to the staff of three Russian institutions: the Russian State Archive for Literature and Art (Moscow), the Manuscript Divisions of the Institute of Russian Literature (St Petersburg) and the Russian State Library (Moscow). I dedicate the book to Robert Louis Jackson, who taught me how to read Dostoevsky and much else besides.

Photo Acknowledgements

The author and publishers wish to express their thanks to the following sources of illustrative material and/or permission to reproduce it:

Photos by the author: pp. 176, 181, 184, 189, 207, 208; Dostoevsky Memorial Museum, St Petersburg: p. 125 (photo B. Taube); Institute of Russian Literature, St Petersburg: pp. 71, 105, 195, 199; Kunstmuseum, Basel: p. 123; Russian State Archive for Literature and Art, Moscow: pp. 106, 130, 135, 141; Russian State Library, Moscow: p. 90; Staatliche Kunstsammlungen, Dresden: pp. 122, 155; State Russian Museum, St Petersburg: pp. 148, 154.